Jaak Rakfeldt
43 Willard St.
New Haven, CT 06515

The Psychotic Patient

The Psychotic Patient

Medication and Psychotherapy

David Greenfeld, M.D.

THE FREE PRESS
A Division of Macmillan, Inc.
NEW YORK

Collier Macmillan Publishers
LONDON

The Free Press
A Division of Macmillan, Inc.
866 Third Avenue, New York, N.Y. 10022

Collier Macmillan Canada, Inc.

Printed in the United States of America

printing number
1 2 3 4 5 6 7 8 9 10

Library of Congress Cataloging in Publication Data

Greenfeld, David.
  The psychotic patient.

  1. Psychoses—Treatment. 2. Psychoses—Chemotherapy.
I. Title. [DNLM: 1. Psychotic Disorders—therapy.
2. Psychotic Disorders—drug therapy. 3. Psychotherapy.
WM 200 G812p]
RC512.G66   1984   616.89′1   84-18775
ISBN 0-02-912830-7

*Dedicated to
the memory of my father*

Contents

Acknowledgments ix

Introduction xi

CHAPTER I. Beginning Treatment 1

CHAPTER II. Outpatient Treatment of Acute Psychosis 17

CHAPTER III. The Therapeutic Alliance 45

CHAPTER IV. Convalescence 63

CHAPTER V. The Assessment of Vulnerability 83

CHAPTER VI. The Meanings of Medication 109

CHAPTER VII. When the Therapist Is Not a Physician 127

CHAPTER VIII. The End of Convalescence 141

Bibliography 181

Index 185

Acknowledgments

FOUR MEN HAVE BEEN particularly important in my development as a psychiatrist. Malcolm Bowers, Psychiatrist-in-Chief of Yale-New Haven Hospital, has managed to combine the roles of boss, mentor, and friend with a skill which has earned my continuing respect and gratitude. Many of the ideas for this work were initially outlined in an article we wrote together. (Bowers and Greenfeld, ''Medication and Psychotherapy in Outpatients Vulnerable to Psychosis,'' in *The Psychotherapy of Schizophrenia*, Strauss, Downey, Fleck, Jackson, and Levine, Eds., Plenum Medical Books, 1980). His clear thinking helped me to sort out some underlying themes in my clinical work and contributed a good deal to the organization and content of this material.

Robert Arnstein, Stephen Fleck, and John Strauss have been my teachers and counselors. In different ways each of them has shaped my thinking and style as a clinician. Each of these four men read earlier drafts of this manuscript, and I have made liberal use of their comments and suggestions in the final version.

I could not have done this work without the enthusiastic support of my wife, Dorothy, and without the tolerant understanding of my children Kimberly, Miranda, and Anna. A special word of thanks is due my secretary Grace Conklin, whose enthusiasm for this project never waned even while typing literally endless drafts. I am also indebted to my friend Benjamin "Steve" Bunney for his critical reading of the final manuscript and to Robert Byck for his assistance in preparing the table on side effects.

Finally, I want to acknowledge my debt to my patients, who continue to teach me daily and who seem to have forgiven most of my many mistakes.

Introduction

AT FIRST GLANCE it might seem that the treatment of patients with psychotic disorders should be simple and straightforward. The introduction of antipsychotic medication has produced a dramatic change in the approach to these patients. Armed with agents that have clearly demonstrated their effectiveness in ameliorating acute psychotic symptoms, clinicians have dramatically reduced the population of mental hospitals, established numerous short-term psychiatric treatment units in the general hospital, and provided effective prophylaxis against recurrent psychosis for a significant portion of psychotically ill patients. A majority of clinicians routinely employ these medications in the treatment of psychotic patients. The judicious use of these agents combined with a program of careful explanation, support, and reassurance should make it possible to manage most psychotically disturbed patients and to protect them against relapse.

Unfortunately, actual clinical experience is more troublesome. The great majority of clinicians, even those most committed to the use of antipsychotic medication, agree that the medication is no panacea. The medication is slow to take effect and it has serious side effects. A period of hospital treatment for acute psychosis is often necessary. Educating, managing, and advising patients is in itself a complex and challenging task. Helping patients with troubling personality deficits, impairments in functioning, and developmental difficulties requires time, effort, and considerable psychotherapeutic skill, and the results are often discouraging.

All too often, the treatment course of patients with psychotic disorders is characterized by periods of recurrent psychosis and by the gradual demoralization and deterioration of the patient. Some patients only respond partially to the medication. Even those who respond optimally still frequently have difficulty. They have trouble with side effects; they refuse to take the medication; or they take it only sporadically. They may ignore diligent attempts to educate them about their disorder, and they may deny illness, reject advice, and refuse treatment. With or without medication, major deficits in their development, personality, and function frequently remain inaccessible to treatment, resulting in continuing suffering and compromise in the quality of life.

The clinicians who face the practical realities of day-to-day treatment of psychotic patients must operate in a pragmatic world of limited time and resources. Most clinicians combine medication and psychotherapy in an attempt to address all aspects of psychotic disorders—the acute symptoms, the chronic deficits in personality and function, the need to educate the patient about his illness and about prophylaxis against recurrent psychosis. Despite the fact that this is now common practice, there is, as yet, no agreement about how these radically different treatment modalities should be integrated into a coherent therapeutic strategy.

What follows is a rough, first approximation of such a proposed strategy. It is not a theoretical document and makes no pretense at being able to unravel the etiology of these disorders or to devise definitive treatment. Rather, it is a practical guide to the clinician who, in the absence of conclusive scientific evidence about optimal treatment of psychotic disorders, is faced with the day-to-day dilemmas of treating suffering patients. The special focus of this work is on the interaction of medication and psychotherapy, attempting to spell out the usual course of treatment and outlining typical problems and priorities at each stage.

Although there is considerable discussion of therapeutic work with family members, the emphasis here is on the treatment of patients who can reasonably be expected to become invested in individual treatment and to use it to help enable them to function independently. The treatment described here is also designed to keep open the possibility of exploratory psychotherapy after the convalescent phase of illness for the minority of patients who can profit from it. The text does not address the treatment of patients who are severely withdrawn, chronically regressed, or very limited in intelligence or motivation.

The text refers to patients suffering from any major psychotic disorder characterized by delusions, hallucinations, or formal thought disorder. It includes the schizophrenic disorders, bipolar disorders, and depressive disorders with psychotic features. Patients suffering from brief reactive or hysterical psychoses, borderline personality disorders, and patients with organic brain disease or major difficulties with substance abuse are sufficiently different to justify their exclusion. The differences between different diagnostic groups of patients are referred to frequently in the body of the text. However, the overriding purpose of this work is to define general principles for combining medication and psychotherapy which can apply to the treatment of all psychotic disorders.

The text assumes that, with rare exception, anyone who suffers from one of the major psychotic disorders will require treatment with neuroleptic medication and/or lithium. It also assumes that such patients will require a period of psychotherapy during their convalescence from the acute episode to assist them in their recovery and to educate them about their disorder. In addition, many patients may require additional psychotherapeutic assistance with difficulties in personality or function. Although patients vary greatly in their need for treatment and their vulnerability to recurrent psychosis, it seems prudent to assume that every patient is at some risk for relapse until events and experience prove otherwise.

The text is not intended to be a complete discussion of treatment. It focuses almost exclusively on the problems of preparing the patient for combined treatment with medication and psychotherapy and on the problems of integrating these modalities. Thus, much of the discussion focuses on early phases of treatment. The often lengthy periods of psychotherapeutic work in which medication plays a minor role are omitted or referred to only briefly. The purpose of this work is to help the experienced clinician with the technical problems generated by combined treatment—with suggestions and illustrations to guide the clinician's thinking and assist him in anticipating and successfully negotiating these common difficulties.

The first three chapters deal with the management of the acute psychotic episode, the initial education of the patient and his family, the problems of establishing a therapeutic alliance, and preparing the patient for subsequent treatment. Chapters 4 through 6 focus on the period of convalescence following the acute episode and on the specific technical problems generated by the combination of medication and psychotherapy. Chapter 7 discusses the special problems which occur when psychotherapy and medication are combined by a clinician who is not a physician. Finally, Chapter 8 discusses the end of the convalescent period, the problem of discontinuing medication, and the transition to more sustained exploratory psychotherapeutic work on the patient's problems in personality and development.

CHAPTER I

Beginning Treatment

ANYONE CONTEMPLATING outpatient treatment of psychotically disturbed patients faces a challenging and often draining prospect. Patients with psychotic disorders suffer wider and more rapid shifts in mood, cognitive state, and capacity to function than most other groups of patients. As a consequence, their therapy requires a broad range of personal resources and technical skills on the part of the clinician. Undertaking such treatment requires a clear awareness of the special needs of these patients, as well as an understanding of the fundamentals which are the underpinnings of all dynamic psychotherapies. Treatment initially requires active, directive, didactic intervention on the part of the therapist as well as the use of antipsychotic medication. The early phases of treatment often involve frequent contact with family members, friends, school authorities, or employers. A period of hospitalization may be neces-

Note: For the purposes of clarity and succinctness, I have chosen to use the masculine pronoun in most instances to refer to both physician and patient. In doing so I wish to make clear that no slight or disrespect for female colleagues and patients is intended.—D.G.

sary at the beginning of treatment and from time to time in later phases as well. Despite these departures from a more familiar, neutral, exploratory stance, the work of understanding these patients draws heavily from dynamic psychotherapeutic principles. Much of the later phases of treatment is essentially exploratory in nature, despite the modifications of technique and style made necessary by the special needs of these patients.

As in any dynamic therapy, useful psychotherapeutic work involves a collaborative effort between patient and therapist from the very beginning of treatment. Although their roles within the treatment are obviously quite different, both parties must participate in a shared effort. This means that any successful treatment will require a well-established alliance, with a genuine dialogue taking place between the patient and therapist. The integrity and quality of this therapeutic relationship is so crucial to treatment that it must always be the first priority of the therapist. Only the threat of immediate danger to the patient or others should take precedence over it. An acutely suicidal or disabled patient may occasionally oblige the clinician to behave in ways that compromise this therapeutic alliance. An acutely psychotic patient may make it necessary for the therapist to abandon a collaborative stance and assume a more directive responsibility for the patient. In the midst of these stressful periods the therapist should keep one eye on the future of the therapeutic relationship and behave with an unfailing commitment to the principle that the patient, no matter how disturbed, is always to be approached with the respect due an equal. For the most part, a thoughtful and well-prepared therapist can manage a crisis in ways that protect the capacity for future therapeutic work with the patient.

Since the therapeutic relationship is at the center of effective treatment from the outset, whatever compromises this relationship compromises the treatment as well. The disintegration of the collaborative aspect of the relationship inevitably leads to a cessation of therapeutic progress and often to the disintegration of the treatment itself. The reader may think it an obvious point that there can be no place in psychotherapy for condescending or patronizing treatment of a patient, no justification for threats, deceptions, or bullying. Unfortunately, the pressures and anxieties associated with the treatment of a psychotic patient can all too frequently lead to just these kinds of damage to trust and rapport. These pressures are particularly, but not exclusively, prominent in the early phases of treatment.

The concepts of confidentiality and informed consent are no less binding for the therapist when the patient is suffering from psychosis. At times the exercise of good clinical judgment may require a therapist to break the rules of confidentiality to safeguard a patient in danger. Similarly, at times the therapist may deem it prudent to defer a full discussion about the benefits and risks of medication until the patient is better able to think clearly about this decision. When these departures from the rules are necessary, they must be conducted with a continuing concern for their possible adverse impact on the therapeutic relationship and every attempt should be made to minimize possible damage to the trust established between clinician and patient. The clinician must explain his actions to the patient, particularly when they involve contact with others. Even a confused and severely disabled patient can often later remember the spirit and tone, if not the specific details of his treatment during a crisis, and that recollection can have a significant impact on subsequent therapeutic work.

Preparation for the Initial Visit

A clinician should attempt to prepare as thoroughly as possible before the initial office visit with the patient. An outpatient therapist may discover, with some surprise, that the patient consulting him for the first time is suffering from psychotic symptoms. More often, however, the clinician knows or strongly suspects that the patient is suffering from psychosis as a result of information or clues available before the first visit. Specifically, the details of the process of referral usually provide useful diagnostic information. In addition to data about the severity of the psychopathology, these details may provide the clinician with valuable clues about the attitudes and motivation of the patient—clues which may help in planning the structure of the patient's initial visit.

The acutely psychotic patient who takes the initiative in making contact and beginning treatment with the outpatient therapist is generally aware (to some degree) that he has psychiatric problems, and by this initiative is indicating his willingness to take a degree of responsibility for his well-being in treatment. On the other hand, when the initiative comes from some other person, that fact suggests that the patient is either unwilling or unable to make the arrangement for himself. The matter is an important one and is well worth the time and effort required to explore it in some detail at the time of referral. When the patient has not called to make the appointment, the therapist should ask the referring person why this is so. The response may be a candid admission that the patient is too frightened, disturbed, or exhausted to come to the telephone. Further exploration with the person calling may yield important information about the severity and nature of the patient's disorder as well as the degree of the patient's reluctance to come for psychiatric consultation. On the basis of this information, the clinician may ask the caller or others to accompany the patient to the consultation or may propose meeting the patient and others at a local emergency room to make an evaluation there.

Occasionally when the therapist attempts to explore why the patient has not called directly, the response may be evasive or guarded. For example, the caller may insist that the patient is "asleep" or "terribly shy with strangers." In instances of this sort, the matter should be gently, but firmly, pressed. For example, if the caller insists that the patient is "asleep," the therapist can insist that the matter is important enough to wake him. Tactful persistence will usually elicit information about the patient's reluctance or inability to come to the telephone or to make the appointment personally. If at all possible it is generally a good idea to speak to the patient, which permits the clinician to get some sense of the patient's capacity to function and to gauge the degree of his resistance to the idea of psychiatric consultation. It also allows the therapist to identify himself, to allay some anxiety, and to be certain that the patient understands that a psychiatric appointment is being made in his behalf (something that cannot always be taken for granted).

When the caller makes it clear that a telephone conversation with the patient is impossible or unwise, it is usually safe to assume that either the patient is refusing treatment or is too ill to converse and the appointment is being made without his knowledge or over his objection in the hope that later he can be persuaded to keep it. The clinician must contain his understandable annoyance at this situation and avoid becoming sharp or judgmental with family members who are less than candid in these initial contacts. They are usually bewildered, frightened, and desperate. Often they are afraid that if they are completely truthful the clinician will refuse to assist them. They are usually also clinging to a frantic denial of the seriousness of the problem and to a dwindling hope that it can be quickly and easily remedied. This common phenomenon is not at all restricted to psychiatric disorders, but is exaggerated with psychotic illness because of the stigma and nightmarish anxiety commonly evoked by psychotic symptoms.

Sources of Referral

The source of referral may be of particular importance in the initial treatment. The route by which a patient comes to treatment can tell the clinician a good deal about the sophistication and attitude of both the patient and family. The referral may come from a wide variety of sources. Patients may reach the clinician through the urging or active intervention of a parent, spouse (or other family member), friend, employer, clergyman, physician, teacher, or via an emergency room—to name the most common. Another group of outpatients may be referred from a psychiatric hospital at or near the time of discharge.

Their acute phase having been managed in an inpatient setting, these patients will enter outpatient treatment having reached the convalescent phase of their illness.

The person making the referral may be a valuable source of information, providing the clinician with information about the patient's clinical condition and about the biases and concerns of both patient and family. When the referral is made by a family physician, the clinician may find him a valuable source of information about the patient's prior history and premorbid functioning. The family doctor may also be able to provide observations about family strengths and problems.

A significant number of psychotically disturbed patients are referred via a hospital emergency room where they have been taken because their illness has become alarming, intolerably distressing, or unmanageable. They may be referred for outpatient treatment because the emergency room clinician determined that the condition was not severe enough to warrant hospitalization. However, a psychotic patient may also be referred because he refused to accept a recommendation of hospitalization and the emergency room physician determined that he was not sufficiently disturbed to warrant involuntary confinement.

Early Manifestations of Denial and Resistance

Patients and their close family members often have a truly astonishing capacity to deny or minimize psychotic symptoms. The psychotic patient and all those close to him may be involved in a search for alternate explanations for symptoms which avoid the painful reality of major psychiatric illness. These alternate explanations may have a degree of plausability and sophistication, depending on the background and circumstances in the particular case. More typically, they range from unlikely to painfully farfetched. In any case, these speculations should never be dismissed out of hand or treated as unworthy of serious discussion. If the immediate crisis is so demanding that time does not permit detailed discussion of these hypotheses, they must be carefully noted for later consideration. A failure to do so may haunt future treatment for many months.

Even the most unlikely of these explanations provides the therapist with some clues as to the sophistication and biases of the patient and those close to him. Most commonly these explanations are ones that conceive of the psychotic disorder as transient and readily cured. Hence, toxic or physical theories are particularly frequent. For example, when the patient is an adolescent with a history of recreational drug use, the family and the patient may insist that LSD or "flashbacks" are producing a "bad trip." All may cling to this explanation long after sufficient time has passed to rule out drugs as anything other than at most an acute precipitant of a major psychotic episode. In instances where the patient has had no history of drug use, other less plausible toxic hypotheses may be advanced. "He was drinking too much coffee" or "he smoked too many cigarettes" may be put forward in all seriousness as causes for psychotic symptoms. "Exhaustion," "overwork," or "not eating right" are also typical (and presumably easily corrected) explanations advanced by both patients and families as causes for major psychiatric symptoms.

Physical illnesses are also common as a proposed explanation—"glandular problems," "hypothyroidism," "hypoglycemia," and "mononucleosis" are typical of illness cited as causes of the frightening symptoms that prompted the psychiatric referral. In many instances the family may have first consulted a family physician or internist in the hopes of clearing up the supposed physical problems underlying the mental symptoms. The fact that the physician has referred the patient for psychiatric treatment does not necessarily insure that the patient or family have abandoned their conviction about the non-psychiatric basis of the disorder. Both the patient and family may be frightened enough to defer to the therapist's judgment during the management of the acute phase of the illness, but their original convictions are likely to resurface once acute symptoms have subsided and some degree of stability has been restored.

Hospitalization versus Outpatient Treatment

Even if the patient is not in an agitated state at the time of the initial visit, he is likely to be extremely anxious, hypervigilant, suspicious, and prone to misinterpret or distort many aspects of the interaction. Despite these difficulties, many acutely psychotic patients can be safely and effectively managed on an outpatient basis and, where this is possible, there is much to recommend it. Outpatient treatment of acute psychosis may speed the process of recovery and avoid the stigma and loss of self-esteem associated with psychiatric hospitalization. On the other hand, outpatient treatment makes it easier for the patient and family to deny the severity of illness and it affords the clinician a much diminished capacity to monitor the evolution of the patient's disorder. Thus, the assessment of the acutely psychotic patient is a critical and continuing requirement in outpatient treatment. Even though a patient is referred for outpatient treatment because a competent clinician determines that symptoms were not severe enough to warrant hospitalization, the therapist must be prepared to reach a different conclusion at any point, based on his own assessment. The patient's condition may deteriorate over a period of days or even hours and a different course of action may be warranted and necessary.

At times the patient is so seriously and dangerously out of control that hospitalization is an obvious immediate necessity. The patient may be so agitated and disruptive, so preoccupied with suicidal or violent impulses, or so severely disabled that a period of treatment in a protected setting is the only prudent alternative. Often, however, the matter is less clearcut and a wide variety of factors must be considered in arriving at the decision to hospitalize. The severity of psychotic symptoms is only one of the many factors that must be weighed carefully.

The presence of hallucinations, delusions, or formal thought disorder are not in themselves sufficient to warrant hospitalization unless they are also dangerous (e.g., command hallucinations) or induce panic (e.g., terrifying persecutory delusions). The degree of the patient's agitation, emotional lability, and the presence of self-destructive or suicidal ideation are also important elements to consider. Other critical factors in deciding about hospitalization include the patient's capacity to form a collaborative alliance with the therapist and the degree of sophistication and responsible concern on the part of the patient's family. Many acutely psychotic patients, though they may be somewhat agitated, confused, and suspicious, are nonetheless capable of recognizing that they are in need of help and of forming a strong alliance with the therapist. On occasion the strength of this alliance is clear during the first interview, where the patient is obviously engaged in a collaborative enterprise with the therapist and is sincerely struggling to be candid and responsible.

If the clinician is considering outpatient treatment of an acutely psychotic patient, a careful discussion with the patient's family is almost always an essential element in assessing its feasibility. Exceptions to this rule include patients who are extremely guarded and suspicious and who insist on controlling the pace of treatment and the level of the therapist's activity. Unless such patients must be subjected to involuntary hospitalization, the clinician has little choice but to gently and patiently suggest courses of action in the hopes that the patient will later accept them.

When the patient does not vigorously object to having family members involved in his treatment, it is important that the clinician determine their skills as observers of the patient's symptoms and behavior. He must assess the strength of their tendency to deny illness and danger and the intensity of their impatience with and fear of the patient. It may also be useful to form some impression about the mental health and stability of members of the patient's family. The presence of a psychotically ill patient at home is bound to produce high anxiety levels and some degree of impaired judgment in even the healthiest of family members. However, if one or more of the patient's immediate family has significant psychiatric illness, outpatient treatment during the acute phase is usually unwise.

It may be particularly important to assess the attitudes of close family members toward not only the patient's symptoms, but toward psychiatric treatment and psychiatric hospitalization as well. Since outpatient treatment of the acutely psychotic patient usually relies heavily on the assistance and support provided by members of the immediate family, the quality of their relationship with the therapist and their ability to form a working alliance is typically a crucial element in outpatient treatment. Family members must share in the treatment responsibility during the acute phase of the illness. They must be both willing and able to do such tasks as taking turns staying with the patient throughout the day, supervising the administration of medication, and reporting to the therapist on changes in the patient's condition.

Discussing Hospitalization

Where hospitalization is a distinct possibility, it is best to introduce the topic early enough to permit considerable time for discussion. Even severely disturbed patients and their families may be surprised and frightened when psychiatric hospitalization is suggested, and the idea frequently generates considerable anxiety and resistance. The recommendation is most easily introduced in the context of a discussion about concerns for the patient's safety. Some patients will be relieved and readily consent to hospitalization, although they may be dismayed at the prospect. The more typical initial reaction is surprise, fear, and a reluctance to consent, despite the severity of symptoms and distress. The therapist may need to do a good deal of educating—both patient and family—about psychiatric hospitals and inpatient treatment, interspersed with considerable reassurance about the prognostic implications of this recommendation. Patients who have never been hospitalized are likely to have distorted and frightening ideas about what psychiatric hospital wards are like and what will happen to them as patients there. For many people television and movies provide the major source of information about psychiatric hospitals, providing a distorted picture which emphasizes the destructive and chaotic aspects of psychiatric hospital treatment. In addition, for many patients and their families the fact of hospitalization is presumed to imply chronic and deteriorating mental illness with all its associated stigma.

A simple and straightforward description of short-term hospital treatment can be extremely helpful, especially if the clinician is familiar with local hospitals and can describe their physical setting, atmosphere, and treatment program in some detail. Since psychotic patients are especially sensitive to rejection, it is also important for the clinician to explain what his relation to the patient would be during hospitalization and to make it clear that he is not attempting to "get rid of" the patient.

Managing the Transition to the Hospital

A patient who has come alone to see the clinician may insist on going home to "pack his bags" or to consult with his family rather than proceed directly to the hospital. Unless this is absolutely inadvisable and dangerous, it is probably best to agree with an understanding that the patient will be in contact with the therapist within a specific time period. Ideally, the therapist can arrange to meet the patient at the hospital at a prearranged time to introduce him to the hospital staff. Even in those instances where the psychiatrist is concerned that going home may be unsafe for the patient, it may be impossible to prevent him from doing so.

In general, it is risky for a psychiatrist to transport an acutely psychotic patient to a hospital in his own automobile unless they have a well-established relationship and the patient is under reasonably good control. Even an apparently willing patient may be highly ambivalent about going to the hospital and it is impossible both to drive an automobile and pay attention to an acutely disturbed patient. On the other hand, several family members may safely transport a willing patient to a nearby hospital. A severely agitated or unmanageable patient requires secure transportation which can be obtained by calling local police or a local ambulance service.

The patient who is opposed to hospitalization presents particular difficulties for the outpatient therapist. Patients are often very reluctant indeed to agree to hospitalization and, not infrequently, adamant in their refusal to accept such a recommendation. Given these facts, it is prudent for the therapist to take a few precautions in considering the need for involuntary hospitalization when evaluating the psychotic patient who has come alone to the clinician's office. For example, it is good practice to obtain the patient's address and phone number early in the interview when such information seems routinely appropriate and before broaching the issue of hospitalization. Such information may be critical if informing the police or the patient's family becomes necessary, and it is almost impossible to force the patient to disclose this information if he is alarmed about possible involuntary commitment. Similarly, the names of employers, school, and family members should be noted as they also may be of great value in an emergency.

The decision to hospitalize a patient involuntarily may occasionally produce enough turmoil and bitterness in the patient to compromise any further therapeutic relationship. The immediate safety of the patient in these instances may be protected at the cost of alienating the patient from the therapist. On rare occasions the experience of involuntary hospitalization may cause the patient to feel such an intense sense of betrayal that he subsequently distrusts all psychotherapists and is inaccessible to treatment. Fortunately, most patients who are confined involuntarily eventually recognize that the action was taken in their best interests. Given the potentially high costs, psychotherapeutically speaking, of involuntary hospitalization, the clinician in some instances may attempt to negotiate a compromise with a psychotic patient who is vehemently opposed to hospitalization and who might be capable of functioning safely outside a hospital. Even though it involves some increased short-term risk for the patient, the clinician might agree to treat the patient on an outpatient basis as long as conditions specified in a carefully planned short-term treatment agreement are met. These situations can be intensely anxiety-provoking for the clinician and less experienced therapists may find it essential to discuss such cases with a supervisor. Short-term agreements of this sort should specify conditions or developments which would be accepted by the patient as indications for voluntary hospitalization.

It *never* makes sense for a therapist to attempt to restrain a patient physically in an outpatient office setting. Unless the clinician is able to muster overwhelming numbers instantly to control a patient physically, it is essential that even implication of physical restraint be avoided. For example, the patient's access to the exit of the consulting room should not be impeded by the placement of the clinician's chair. One individual can never safely restrain a psychotic patient and the attempt to do so increases the risk of panic and injury, making the permanent alienation of the patient from the therapist extremely likely. On the other hand, it sometimes helps to gain time by attempting to persuade the patient to remain in the office and discuss matters further.

Occasionally, a therapist may find that he is so concerned about a patient's safety that he attempts to persuade the patient to remain in his office while waiting for secure transportation to a psychiatric hospital. If the patient strongly objects, the atmosphere may become tense and the patient may become panicky and agitated. Sometimes such a patient can be detained by stern insistence that he remain where he is. This tactic may work for a while, but it is risky and may increase the tension to an unmanageable point. It is better to be open and direct with patients in such circumstances, making it clear what will happen should they adopt a particular course of action. For example, if the patient asks "What will you do if I run out of the office?'' the clinician can respond by saying, ''I would not attempt to stop you, but I would be alarmed enough to call your family and tell them I was concerned for your safety.'' Of course, the clinician should make a statement of this sort only if he is genuinely concerned enough to carry out the action described. If a fleeing patient appears to be a danger to himself or others or is gravely disabled, the police and family members can be contacted and the clinician can arrange to meet the patient at a local emergency room for certification to a psychiatric hospital for observation.

Given the difficulties and uncertainties in making the decision to hospitalize an acutely psychotic patient, it is inevitable that mistakes will be made. It is probably best for less experienced clinicians to lean toward hospitalization as the safer course. Fortunately, as the following case illustrates, patients often let the attentive clinician know if the decision was a poor one.

> A 24-year-old graduate student was brought to the emergency room of a local hospital by his roommates because he had become extremely anxious, hyperactive, and delusional. He seemed aware that he was in some psychological difficulty and he calmed down after several hours in the emergency room. He denied suicidal ideation and seemed confident that his living situation with his roommates was a supportive and helpful one. He adamantly refused psychiatric hospitalization and, since his roommates agreed to help look after him on a short-term basis, he was referred for prompt outpatient assessment and treatment. His outpatient psychiatrist saw him the same day and proposed an acute treatment plan involving antipsychotic medication and frequent outpatient visits. The patient agreed to this plan, but as he was leaving his therapist's office he turned and said ''You know, doctor, when I look at you I see Life, but when I look outside this door I see Death.'' The therapist invited him back into the office for further discussion and suggested that he might feel safer in a hospital setting. Although still hesitant and suspicious, the patient soon agreed to inpatient treatment with relief.

While careful assessment and disposition of the patient are inevitably the central concerns of the clinician during the initial sessions, the engagement of the patient and family in treat-ment is at least equally important to its ultimate success. The most astute diagnosis and disposition are of little value if the experience leaves the patient and family confused, frightened, and alienated from the clinician.

CHAPTER II

Outpatient Treatment of Acute Psychosis

FOR MANY ACCUTELY PSYCHOTIC PATIENTS treatment can only be conducted safely in an inpatient setting. For these patients, outpatient treatment begins when psychotic symptoms have subsided and convalescence has begun. However, when conditions are favorable there may be distinct advantages to treating an acutely psychotic patient outside a psychiatric hospital. Outpatient management can minimize regression and help avoid much of the humiliation and loss of self-esteem associated with psychiatric hospitalization. On occasion outpatient treatment may be necessary even if circumstances are less than favorable, for example if resources are limited or if the patient and family are vehemently opposed to hospitalization.

The safe management and protection of the patient must be the clinician's primary concern during the acute psychotic period. Hence, outpatient treatment is limited to those patients whose psychotic symptoms present no immediate serious danger or management difficulty and who are able to take some degree of responsibility for cooperation in their treatment. Outpatient treatment is greatly facilitated if the patient is compliant, responds well to medication, and has an involved, supportive, and cooperative network of family and/or friends.

After safe management and protection of the patient, the
central therapeutic task is the suppression and control of acute
psychotic symptoms, usually through the administration of
antipsychotic medication. With rare exception, consent to the
use of medication is an essential part of outpatient management of acute psychosis. However, the patient may (tacitly) in-
tend this consent to apply only to the period of acute crisis and
the continued use of medication may need to be renegotiated
once the crisis has subsided. When acute psychotic symptoms
are safely under control, the resulting stability permits a more
detailed and thoughtful treatment plan to be discussed.

Approaching the Acutely Psychotic Patient

Outpatient treatment of acutely psychotic patients is a specialized form of crisis intervention and as such requires a high level
of involvement, activity, and availability on the part of the clinician. Acutely pscyhotic patients are usually frightened, bewildered, and hyperalert. Some are guarded, taciturn, and suspicious, while others talk freely, describing bizarre ideas and
experiences in great detail. The combination of psychotic illness and the anxiety associated with initial therapeutic contact
makes such patients extremely sensitive to stimuli of all sorts.
A hyperalert patient is likely to be aware of normally over-
looked details and nuances of the interaction with the clinician
and may distort or misinterpret their significance. Acutely psychotic patients vary greatly in their capacity to relate to the clinician. Some patients can talk in a calm and organized way
about delusional preoccupations, but many others are rambling
and incoherent, pressured and emotionally labile. Whatever
the clinical presentation, a psychotic patient may be suitable for
outpatient treatment if he is not out of control and a supportive
environment can be structured to tide him over the acute crisis.
Patients who are very agitated, who have high energy levels or
who show evidence of marked impulsivity are generally poor
candidates for outpatient treatment. Consequently, manic patients are often too difficult to manage in an outpatient setting.

In approaching the acutely psychotic patient, the most effective stance for the clinician is one of calm, sensitive attention. Appropriate expressions of sympathy or concern should be clearly communicated but muted in intensity. Since acutely psychotic patients are typically very distractible, the clinician should keep his comments brief and simple. If a patient is very disorganized and incoherent (or nearly so), there is little point in allowing him to ramble on endlessly. A patient whose speech tumbles out in a disorganized cascade may be politely interrupted with structuring and clarifying questions. The clinician can explain to the patient that he seems confused and is difficult to understand. A patient who responds well to these interventions may also be able to recognize that his speech is very rapid and disorganized if this is called to his attention.

For the most part, acutely psychotic patients are truthful in what they say, but the clinician should remember that they often omit important information if it is not asked for directly. Thus, it is essential that each patient be asked candidly about suicidal thoughts or acts and about fears of panic or losing control. Evasive, ambiguous, or confused responses must be explored with persistent, simple, direct questions until each of these matters is sufficiently clear to the clinician. Guarded patients may, at times, actively conceal and deny delusions or hallucinations, thereby making it difficult to determine if they are in immediate danger or in need of hospitalization. These patients never respond to pressure or badgering. The clinician may have little choice but to assume that a patient who is able to conceal psychotic symptoms successfully is sufficiently in control of himself to manage safely outside a hospital setting.

The Short-Term Treatment Agreement

Outpatient treatment of acute psychosis is governed by a short-term agreement designed to meet and manage the crisis posed by the patient's acute symptoms. Once the clinician has decided that outpatient treatment is a possibility, he and the patient must see if agreement can be reached about the conditions under which the treatment will be conducted. Any such agreement may need frequent revision, since acute psychotic symptoms can intensify or change at any point in the acute phase. The short-term agreement evolves day by day, both explicitly and implicitly as circumstances warrant. The agreement gradually defines crisis treatment goals and the special arrangements designed to facilitate treatment until a period of relative calm and stability is restored.

During the acute treatment period, whenever the safety of the patient is at stake it is incumbent upon the therapist to be certain that the short-term agreement is a firm and reliable one. While absolute certainty is, of course, impossible, the therapist should make clear that the patient has the burden of convincing the therapist that the agreement is reliable. The therapist should reject any tentative or doubting expressions about the agreement on the part of the patient. Statements such as ''I will try to keep this agreement'' or ''I think I can do it'' or any other expression conveying doubt or uncertainty should be questioned and challenged by the therapist. The patient should be reminded that successful collaboration in this kind of treatment plan requires the patient's assurance that he can carry out his part of the agreement. Even a moderate degree of hesitancy or uncertainty on the part of the patient about issues crucial to his safety should be taken as evidence that such an outpatient plan is unwise. If uncertainty cannot be resolved relatively promptly, the clinician should either modify the plan or shift to a recommendation for inpatient care.

The patient must agree to his family's involvement in acute outpatient treatment. In general, it is best if the patient is present when the therapist talks with members of the family, since the treatment plan must be agreed to by all concerned and the patient should understand that the therapist will discuss his behavior with family members during this phase. Whenever the patient is not present when contact occurs between the patient's family and the therapist (e.g., phone contact), the patient should be given an accurate summary of the contact on the next occasion when patient and therapist meet.

When the opportunity arises, the clinician should take the opportunity to explain to both patient and family the clinician's obligation to avoid either the fact or appearance of dishonesty or deception. At the same time, the patient's privacy must be respected and information not necessary to the safe management of the patient must remain confidential. Thus, when a family member attempts to make use of contact with the therapist to inquire into details of the patient's history, the clinician should make it clear that these matters cannot be discussed.

The short-term treatment plan may involve frequent sessions and frequent telephone contact with both the patient and members of his family. Daily visits and/or telephone contacts may be necessary initially, and their focus should be invariably the management of the patient's condition and symptoms. As the patient's condition stabilizes the frequency of meetings and telephone contacts can be decreased gradually. If outpatient treatment goes well, the acute psychotic symptoms may be controlled to some degree in a few days, and the patient often can be adequately stabilized within a few weeks. On occasion, however, adequate control may take considerably longer. Until such control is achieved, the patient's condition can change rapidly and unpredictably and therefore requires careful monitoring. The family also requires monitoring during this period, since the management of an acutely psychotic patient is extremely stressful and the endurance of family members may be limited. If the patient's progress is too slow and the family is becoming exhausted, hospitalization may be necessary.

Acute Outpatient Treatment

Outpatient treatment of an acutely psychotic patient is always stressful and often turbulent for all concerned. The unpredictable development of frightening and intensely painful symptoms in the patient challenges the clinician's ability to remain calm and thoughtfully professional. The therapist must pay careful attention to his own anxiety level, since it can be of great assistance in the continuing reassessment this treatment requires. If the therapist finds he is growing increasingly anxious about a patient's safety, it usually means that some carefully considered action is necessary, perhaps simply consulting with a colleague about the case. More often it may prompt the clinician to reconsider some aspect of the treatment plan or make some other direct intervention lessening the level of concern.

It is essential that the therapist's actions not be hasty, impulsive, or arbitrarily imposed on the patient without careful discussion and mutual consent. High levels of anxiety may tempt the therapist to engage in battles with the patient or to adopt a disrespectfully assertive, controlling, or condescending attitude. A frightened and insecure clinician may bully or threaten a patient, engage in arguments or appeals to authority, or resort to intimidating psychiatric jargon. Even when these interventions have the desired short-term result, they are apt to do lasting damage to the therapeutic alliance and may permanently alienate the patient.

The acutely psychotic patient is *not* a suitable candidate for exploratory psychotherapy; in fact such activity is contraindicated. Even when the psychotic decompensation occurs in the midst of an exploratory phase of treatment, the exploration of the events surrounding the decompensation must be deferred until the patient's psychotic symptoms have been controlled. On the other hand, the clinician's skill at managing the acute crisis can do a great deal to enhance the therapeutic alliance and therefore the quality of subsequent treatment. Insensitive management of a crisis can severely compromise treatment, although the effect may be delayed for many months, often until the end of convalescence. The clinician who can safely, calmly, and effectively guide a patient through an acute psychotic crisis has gone a long way toward establishing his expertise and authority with regard to subsequent treatment issues. Ideally, the therapist is able to deal safely with the acute crisis while protecting the working relationship with the patient and assessing the potential impact of each intervention on the therapeutic alliance.

The clinician may give a good deal of practical advice to his patient concerning short-term management of his affairs during the crisis. Indeed, the degree of impairment in the patient's judgment combined with the distress and anxiety in close family members make it necessary for the clinician to behave as a knowledgeable expert who guides the patient and his family through the crisis. The clinician must take care not to exploit this authority and must eschew opinions on any major life decisions or on longer term treatment issues.

At times the clinician may need to intervene actively with employers or school authorities to protect a patient's job or academic standing. Often the patient's performance has been deteriorating for a period of time. The patient may have been overtly disturbed in the school or work setting, and it may be important for the clinician to listen to an employer or teacher at some length to reassure them that the behavior and problems described were the result of a treatable illness and that the patient can be expected to return eventually to premorbid levels of function. These interventions can help to reduce the patient's fears and relieve him of the necessity of having to make explanations directly to a boss or teacher. While the patient must give his general consent to contacts of this sort, it may not be possible or practical to obtain his specific consent for each disclosure made by the clinician during a rapidly developing crisis. In such instances it should be made clear to the patient that he is giving the therapist the authority to use his best judgment in each instance. The therapist, in turn, should be guided by the principle that he discloses the absolute minimum of information necessary to protect the patient's interests during the acute crisis.

Beginning the Educational Process

While preoccupied with managing acute psychotic symptoms, as well as protecting and nurturing his relationship with the patient, the clinician must somehow begin the task of educating the patient and family about the illness and its treatment.

As the crisis subsides the patient and family must be prepared to transform an active, crisis-oriented treatment into a stable and regular ongoing treatment much different in tone and character—a treatment with different rules, practices, and goals. Information is best presented in simple, clear language. All psychiatric jargon should be avoided. Spreading small, digestable amounts of information throughout the treatment at frequent intervals is usually a very effective technique, as is simply providing clear explanations about each aspect of the treatment as it unfolds, including a few sentences of relevant background to help the patient and family form a clear conception of the psychotic illness and its treatment.

The therapist's efforts at educating patient and family are complicated by the fact that all are preoccupied with the acute crisis and are usually unable to be attentive and thoughtful. Patients and families typically have much difficulty retaining information about all aspects of the patient's illness and treatment, so the clinician patiently should repeat important points and expect that critical information frequently will be distorted or forgotten altogether. The therapist can learn something about the degree of difficulty the patient and his family are having in absorbing this information by encouraging them to express their opinions about the patient's illness and treatment. The educational process is enhanced considerably if the patient and family have the opportunity to discuss their views at some length and to pinpoint major areas of disagreement with the therapist.

In the early phases of treatment these differences tend to center around two global issues: the character and severity of the patient's illness and the nature of the treatment required. At times these differences may be expressed by strong divergence of opinion about the use of antipsychotic medication. The patient's and family's need to minimize the serverity of psychotic illness is understandable and quite common, and it accounts, in part, for the frequency with which patients and families postpone psychiatric consultation until psychotic symptoms are alarmingly severe. During the acute phase of treatment the wish to minimize and deny the patient's illness is commonly manifested in the tendency to view the crisis intervention as the whole of treatment, with the hope that such brief intervention will leave the patient "cured" and "normal." Having been forced to face the fact of serious psychiatric illness which requires immediate treatment, the patient and family frequently insist on viewing the illness as an isolated episode unrelated to the patient's premorbid life or character and thus requiring only the management and suppression of symptoms.

Oddly enough, the use of antipsychotic medication may make it easier for the patients and families to adopt this "isolated episode" view. A rapid response to antipsychotic medication may make it more likely that the patient and his family will minimize and distort the severity of the psychotic episode. Because of the intensity of their need to deny the seriousness of the psychotic illness, patients and families have a tendency to regard these early improvements as the result of spontaneous remission, thus affirming their belief that the illness is transient, self-limiting, and comparatively minor. They are inclined to be skeptical of the role the antipsychotic medication played in the remission of symptoms, regarding it instead as a powerful (and possibly addicting) "tranquilizer" or "sedative." They see the medication as providing some calming effect while the "spontaneous remission" takes place. The popular media's depiction of the use of antipsychotic medication often fosters the idea that the medication acts primarily as a "tranquilizer."

These or similar views frequently lead the patient and his family to experiment with prematurely reducing the dosage of antipsychotic medications. The longer the patient is comparatively symptom-free, the greater the temptation to regard the medication as unnecessary. It is only by encouraging the frank discussion of opinions about all aspects of treatment that the clinician can begin educating the patient and his family about the complex treatment task they have begun. The therapist should expect considerable resistance to his educational efforts, since he is presenting the disturbing fact that psychosis is a serious disorder which will require a period of treatment after acute symptoms are resolved and which may require intensive, expensive, and comparatively prolonged treatment as well. Like all resistance in psychotherapy, this type also should be approached with tact and patience.

In the early stages of treatment both the patient and family need frequent reminders that the acute treatment is designed to control symptoms and to establish stability in order that possible contributing problems and stresses can be identified and addressed in a less pressured and turbulent atmosphere. Similarly, when antipsychotic medication is introduced into the treatment, it should be clearly identified as an agent designed to suppress certain symptoms and, in conjuction with psychotherapy, to protect the patient against relapse. In this way the patient and family can be introduced gradually to two concepts central to the treatment of psychotic illness: (1) the concept of psychosis as a complex entity requiring a varied and complex treatment aimed at different dimensions of the illness and (2) the concept of vulnerability to recurrent psychosis and the need to evolve a strategy to minimize that vulnerability.

Explaining the Purpose of Medication

It is important that the patient and his family understand that the medications are agents designed to control specific symptoms and that they are not "tranquilizers". It is especially helpful to identify several specific target symptoms that can be recognized and acknowledged. Then, the patient and family can monitor the target symptoms as they respond to antipsychotic drug treatment. However, the clinician may be surprised to find that obvious psychotic symptoms are denied not only by the patient, but by family members as well. It often requires considerable patience and persistence to identify and label target symptoms that can be mutually agreed upon and jointly monitored. Target symptoms are best described in simple everyday language, avoiding technical terms and jargon. Terms such as "hallucinations," "loose associations," "delusions," and the like are more often alarming than helpful. Their use often requires elaborate explanation and reassurance and may intensify denial and resistance. Target symptoms can be usefully described with adequate precision as "disorganization," "having strange thoughts," "difficulties thinking clearly," "confusion," "feeling panicky," "difficulties with concentration," "hearing voices," "severe nervousness," or the like. With some cautious exploration and attentive listening, the clinician will soon learn which words are acceptable to describe the patient's symptoms. The goal in this early stage is to define a rationale for the use of antipsychotic medication which can enlist the cooperation and support of the patient and family without forcing them to confront fully the severity of the patient's psychotic illness. In addition, it helps the patient to monitor the effects of the medication and thus to enlist his active collaboration in using the medication as a central element in treatment.

The clinician should discuss the potential benefits and risks of the medication, if possible, before initiating the treatment. Informed consent is an essential part of the education the clinician must provide. However, in many instances a detailed discussion of possible risks is best deferred until the immediate crisis has subsided. Preoccupied and frantic family members may not be in a position to make reasoned and balanced judgments about the use of medication and the responsibility for such a decision may add to their distress. In these instances the clinician must take care to initiate a discussion of risks at the earliest suitable moment in the patient's convalescence from the acute episode.

The clinician should take advantage of any opportunity to continue the education of the patient. This can be done by providing clear explanations about the purposes of each proposed change in medication, anticipating future changes, and preparing the patient for them. For example, when discussing a current change in dosage the patient can be reminded that the dosage will eventually be lowered once the symptoms have subsided, thus reinforcing the idea that medication will be continued after acute symptoms are under control. Emotionally charged or highly conflicted therapeutic issues which arise during this acute period can be identified and then deferred for later consideration when a degree of stability has been achieved. The therapist can clarify this process by explaining that the immediate goal of treatment is to gain control of symptoms and to make the situation manageable and safe. The therapist can indicate that once such a period of stability is established the treatment will shift in its focus and address important preexisting problems.

In practice it is usually impossible during the acute phase of treatment to educate the patient and family fully or even adequately about the complexities of psychotherapy and antipsychotic medication. The educational process is a slow one which can only begin during this phase and must continue throughout the treatment. Even when both the patient and family appear fully compliant and sophisticated about these matters, the clinician must be prepared to review each of these points once the crisis has subsided. No matter how seemingly effective the therapist's efforts have been at educating the patient and family about antipsychotic medication, the therapist must also be prepared to learn that the patient and family have only consented to short-term use of medication and wish to reopen discussions about the need to continue maintenance medication. At this point a new agreement must be negotiated defining prophylactic and rehabilitative treatment goals. This can rarely be done in a single session and it must be worked on repeatedly as the patient's acute symptoms subside and he enters a period of convalescence.

Resistance to Medication and Compliance Problems in the Acute Phase

One can never confidently assume that a psychotic patient will follow instructions with regard to antipsychotic medication. Even when a patient and family readily consent to the use of medication, it cannot be assumed that they are free of misgivings, misconceptions, and reservations concerning its use. Unexplored, these misgivings may lead them to misinterpret or unilaterally modify dosage instructions as the patient's clinical condition changes.

When neither the patient nor family are vehemently opposed to its use, it is usually possible to explore their concerns and reservations about antipsychotic medication and to reassure them enough to begin a medication trial. In addition to discussing the concerns raised by the patient and family, it is usually wise to consider in advance common side effects to avoid surprise and unnecessary anxiety. Thus, patients should be warned about possible sedation, blurring of vision, dry mouth, and constipation. Potential interactions with drugs and alcohol should be described and patients must be cautioned against their use, and on the dangers of driving and operating machinery during the initial treatment period. Once the dosage of medication is lowered to maintainance levels it is safe for most patients to drink in moderation. However, hallucinogenic drugs are dangerous for psychotic patients and should be avoided indefinitely. Some patients are able to use marijuana safely in moderation, but it is probably best to avoid it altogether.

Some useful preliminary information about the patient's attitude toward the use of medication can be obtained while taking his history. The patient should always be asked if he has taken any psychotropic medication in the past. Besides being information of value in its own right, the tone and spirit of the patient's responses often provide important clues to his likely reaction to the recommendation that he take antipsychotic medication. For example, the patient who responds to a question about possible past medication use with a tense and abrupt, "I would never take tranquilizers. I think they do lasting damage," is someone who will need considerable preparation and education before feeling comfortable about taking antipsychotic medication. Even those patients whose response is generally favorable to the idea of medication may show subtly that they are frightened of medication and suspicious about its effects. Patients whose fears about the effects of anti-psychotic medication are not adequately explored may later ex-press these fears by focusing their anxieties with great intensity on minor side effects.

When clinically effective doses of antipsychotic medication are administered, the risk of dystonic reactions is significant. The clinician should forewarn both patient and family about the possibility of these reactions in the first few days of treat-ment and describe the symptoms clearly. It may be helpful to provide a family member with a small supply of antiparkinson medication to keep in readiness at home so that dystonic symp-toms can be treated promptly, should they occur. If the patient is able to continue to work or to attend school, prophylactic treatment with antiparkinson agents may be advisable. This is especially true for younger patients, since dystonic reactions are more common in adolescents and young adults. An acute dystonic reaction may cause a patient severe difficulty and em-barrassment if it occurs at work, at school, or in the commu-nity. The result of such an episode may be an intense distrust of medication and a significant setback in the treatment, as in the following example.

An 18-year-old woman was referred for outpatient treatment of an acute psychotic disorder. Although she was moderately disor-ganized, irritable, extremely anxious, and distractable, she was able to continue her work as a file clerk with some difficulty. She readily agreed to take antipsychotic medication and was begun on a moderate dose of perphenazine with good clinical effect. How-ever, on the third day of treatment she had a severe dystonic reac-tion while driving her car through the countryside. She was able to pull off the road to a shopping area but as soon as she got out of her car she was unable to speak. She was taken by ambulance to the emergency room of a nearby community hospital where she remained for five hours until a neurologist could be summoned to make the appropriate diagnosis and institute treatment. As a result of this experience the patient refused to take medication for several months. The distrust engendered by this experience ex-tended beyond medication to include the treatment and the therapist himself. The content of psychotherapeutic hours during the several months following this incident were largely occupied with a review of the incident and its consequences. The therapeutic alliance was restored to its former level only after considerable time-consuming effort.

Prophylactic treatment with antiparkinson medication may also be advisable for some paranoid patients or for patients who are very hesitant about taking antipsychotic medication, since a dystonic reaction may prompt these individuals to refuse medication thereafter. When used to control the side effects of antipsychotic agents, antiparkinson medications should be tapered slowly once the dose of antipsychotics is stabilized. In most cases the antiparkinson medications can be discontinued altogether after two or three months.

Choosing a Medication

There is no good evidence that any neuroleptic agent is more effective than any other in treating a particular psychotic symptom and there is little reason to prescribe more than one of these agents at a time. The antipsychotic agents differ primarily in their potency and side effect profile. Therefore, the clinician should choose a medication with these facts in mind and should be familiar with a suitable variety of agents. The treatment of acute psychosis usually requires a rapid increase in the dosage of medication to fairly high levels in order to control acute psychotic symptoms. Once the patient is stable and symptoms are adequately controlled, the medication can gradually be reduced to maintenance levels. On occasion, a highly suspicious or resistant patient may need to be treated with small doses of medication which are very gradually increased to effective antipsychotic levels. This strategy may permit the clinician to reassure the patient over a period of time that the medication is safe and does not produce frightening or unexpected effects. The very gradual increase in dosage can reduce the likelihood of sudden onset of severe side effects which might prompt the patient to discontinue the medication altogether.

Also, the clinician should consider the cost of medication. Some antipsychotic medications are quite expensive and for many patients this may be an important factor which affects compliance with the regimen. The therapist can check with local pharmacies about the prices of different medications and in some instances prescribing choices may be influenced by financial considerations as much as by other factors. Maintenance dosage schedules should be tailored as much as possible to suit the patient's convenience, if possible consolidating all of the doses into a single one at bedtime. This schedule enhances compliance since the patient is less likely to forget the medication, while taking advantage of whatever sedative effect the medication produces to enhance the patient's sleep. When a single dose at bedtime is not desirable, the daily dosage can be divided into morning and bedtime doses with little loss in compliance. Most patients have difficulty remembering more than two doses of a medication daily and such schedules should be avoided if at all possible.

Early Subjective Reactions to Antipsychotic Medication

The patient's initial reactions to the first doses of medication are extremely important. These first impressions often persist indefinitely and therefore can provide the clinician with crucial information about the patient's likely attitude toward that particular medication (and possibly toward antipsychotic medication in general) during all of future treatment. To assess the patient's initial reaction it is particularly important that the clinician show an early sympathetic interest in the patient's subjective response to the medication, taking the patient's opinions seriously despite the fact that he or she is suffering from florid psychotic symptoms. By demonstrating sincere interest in the patient's response, the clinician helps to establish early

TABLE 1. Commonly Prescribed Neuroleptics

Antipsychotic Agents	Estimated Equivalent Dose*	Typical Outpatient Maintenance Dosage mg/day	Side Effects				
			SEDATION	EXTRA-PYRAMIDAL SYMPTOMS	HYPOTENSION	ANTI-CHOLINERGIC ACTIVITY	
PIPERIDINE Thioridazine (Mellaril)	100	50–250	High	Low	High	High	
ALIPHATIC Chlorpromazine (Thorazine)	100	50–250	High	Moderate	High	High	
PIPERAZINE Perphenazine (Trilafon)	10	12–24	Moderate	High	Low	Moderate	
Trifluoperazine (Stelazine)	5	4–10	Low	High	Low	Low	
Fluphenazine (Prolixin)	2	1–5	Low	High	Low	Low	
THIOXANTHENE Thiothixene (Navane)	5	5–30	Low	Moderate	Moderate	Low	
BUTYROPHENONES Haloperidol (Haldol)	2	2–10	Low	High	Low	Low	

*Approximate antipsychotic potency of each agent equivalent to an arbitrary standard of chlorpromazine = 100 (e.g., 2 mg haloperidol ≅ 100mg chlorpromazine).

in treatment a collaborative and mutually respectful approach to a medication regimen and an atmosphere in which a patient may confide opinions candidly.

For some patients the initial reaction to medication is largely positive. Although these patients may complain about side ef-

TABLE 2. Clinically Significant Drug Interactions with Neuroleptics

Drug Interacting with Neuroleptics	Clinical Effect of Interaction
Anticholinergics	Increased anticholinergic effect
Narcotics	Increased sedation Augmented analgesia Augmented hypotension Augmented respiratory depression Anticholinergic effects augmented by meperidine
Cyclic antidepressants	Increased sedation Increased anticholinergic effect
L-dopa	Decreased antiparkinson effect May exacerbate psychosis
Barbiturates Nonbarbiturate hypnotics	Increased sedation Decreased clinical effect of neuroleptic
Amphetamines	May exacerbate psychosis
Iproniazid	Hepatic toxicity and encephalopathy Decreased neuroleptic effect
Reserpine Clonidine Guanethidine Bethanidine Debrisoquine	Decreased antihypertensive effect
Epinephrine	Hypotension augmented
Insulin Oral antidiabetic drugs	Neuroleptics increase blood glucose and may alter required dose of diabetic medication

Note: Information in Tables 2 and 3 loosely based on Salzman, Carl, and Hoffman, Steven A., Clinical Interaction Between Psychotropic and Other Drugs. *Hospital and Community Psychiatry*, October 1983, 34, *10*, pp. 897–902.

**TABLE 3.   Clinically Significant Drug
Interactions with Lithium**

Drug Interacting with Lithium	*Clinical Effect of Interaction*
Methyldopa	Increased lithium toxicity
Indomethacin Piroxicam Sulindac Ibuprofen Phenylbutazone Naproxen Zomepirac	Increased lithium effect and toxicity due to decreased renal lithium clearance
Theophylline Acetazolamide Aminophylline	Increased renal excretion of lithium decreasing its effect
Succinylcholine Pancuronium Decamethonium	Prolonged apnea with electroconvulsive therapy
Thiazide diuretics Phenylbutazone Spironolactone Triamterene Amiloride	Increased lithium effect and toxicity due to increased tubular reabsorption of lithium
Sodium bicarbonate Urea Mannitol	Increased renal excretion of lithium decreasing its effect
Sodium Chloride (table salt)	Large doses increase lithium excretion and reduce blood levels. Low salt diet may increase lithium blood levels and toxicity
Tetracycline Spectinomycin	Increased lithium effect and toxicity due to depressed renal lithium clearance
Haloperidol	Very rare occurrence of delirium and/or encephalopathy
Furosemide	Increased lithium toxicity resulting from sodium depletion
Insulin	Insulin dosage may need adjustment early in lithium treatment due to altered glucose tolerance

fects, they are also aware that the overall effect of the medication is helpful and that their mental state is improved. These patients appear to value the medication from the outset and seem to have some grasp of its importance in their treatment. Although they may resist taking medication and express a wish to decrease or discontinue it because of their displeasure with side effects, such patients will usually negotiate these matters with an interested and involved clinician.

Other patients have a clear, strongly negative reaction to the early experience of the medication. These patients may express this negative reaction by focusing on unpleasant side effects such as sedation, blurred vision, or extrapyramidal symptoms. At times side effects can be particularly uncomfortable, so much so that the patient finds the medication intolerable. Akathisia is frequently especially unpleasant for the patient, even in cases where it appears relatively trivial to the clinician. The patient's restlessness may at times be apparent and can easily be mistaken for agitation or anxiety. However, even when the patient appears relatively calm, he may still be suffering from a subjective state of restlessness or unease due to a subtle akathisia which may be distressing enough to make him resolutely opposed to taking the medication. Patients are often inarticulate about these discomforts and may describe them in incoherent or unfocused ways. The clinician may need to question the patient carefully and specifically to get the facts clear. A trial of antiparkinson medication may be helpful in making the diagnosis of akathisia, particularly if the medication is administered intramuscularly. However, for some patients even the addition of antiparkinson agents to the treatment regimen is not sufficient to relieve this distressing symptom. A reduction in the dosage of medication or a change to a different antipsychotic medication may be necessary if the patient is to remain an active collaborator in treatment.

While an early strongly negative response to antipsychotic medication may result from discomfort due to side effects, for some patients this sort of response is a subjective reaction to the primary effect of the medication on the patient's thinking and mental activity. Reactions of this sort can occur even if the patient appears to have improved greatly as a result of treatment with the medication and appears to be free of significant side effects. These patients will report that the medication has made them worse, even though they may appear to the clinician to be dramatically improved. Patients often have difficulty describing reactions of this sort, but they usually manage to convey a sense of feeling blunted, numbed, drugged, or painfully or unnaturally changed. "I'm not myself," "my thinking is slowed way down," "I feel I can't think right," "it makes me feel dull," are typical of the comments patients make when they react in this way. Other patients may resent the loss of grandiose or pleasurable delusions, euphoric mood, or other intense and exciting symptoms and they may find the nonpsychotic state unpalatable in comparison. These negative reactions should be taken seriously by the clinician, since these patients are very likely to discontinue the medication at the earliest opportunity. Although they can sometimes be persuaded to continue medication during the acute phase of illness despite their subjective response, a drastic reduction in the dosage may be necessary if the patient is to be maintained on medication as an outpatient. In some instances where the distress is particularly severe, low doses of intermittent medication may be the only way to maintain the patient in treatment at all.

Nathan, a 22-year-old single man, lives at home with his parents and works the night shift at a factory. He has been hospitalized three times for psychotic illness characterized by social withdrawal, paranoid delusions, and auditory hallucinations. The first psychotic episode occurred while he was a college student and resulted in a hospital stay of two months. He attempted to return to college the following year but suffered a recurrence of psychotic symptoms. Since his second hospitalization he has lived at home and worked in a factory. Although he is withdrawn and isolated he has managed to work consistently, suffering only one additional exacerbation of psychotic symptoms which required hospitalization.

Nathan strongly dislikes antipsychotic medication and usually refuses to take it. During each of his last two hospitalizations the nurses discovered that he was cheeking medications. Although he acknowledges that the medication reduces the severity of his symptoms, he does not regard this as an improvement. He feels the medication is dangerous and unpleasant, describing its effect as "someone throwing a blanket over my mind." Although he has been intermittently in outpatient psychotherapy, he has always discontinued his medications shortly after discharge from the hospital.

Although he knows that "something is wrong," Nathan does not believe that he has a psychiatric illness. On those occasions when his psychotic symptoms become severe, he has allowed himself to be taken to a hospital emergency room by his parents and at their urging he has reluctantly signed himself into the hospital.

During Nathan's third hospitalization considerable time and energy was devoted to negotiating an agreement with him regarding his outpatient treatment. The agreement specified that his parents could monitor his condition and report to his therapist when his symptoms were becoming more marked or were interfering with his ability to work or get along at home. At those times his parents would accompany him to his session with his therapist and discuss their concerns. If his parents and therapist both felt it was necessary, Nathan would agree to take low doses of antipsychotic medication for limited periods of time. He would permit his parents to administer the medication and check to be sure that he was not cheeking the pills. It also was agreed that when his therapist and parents determined that his behavior at home had improved he would be permitted to discontinue the medication.

This arrangement represented a compromise for all parties, and all considered it less than optimal. However, it permitted Nathan to remain in treatment and to continue his factory work. Although both his family and his therapist repeatedly encouraged him to continue the medication beyond these short-term periods, Nathan invariably refused to do so.

Whatever the initial reaction to antipsychotic medication, the clinician's early and continuing interest in the patient's feelings and opinions is essential if the patient is to become an active collaborator in treatment. During the early weeks of treatment with antipsychotics many patients can tolerate a period of dysphoria if the clinician is clearly concerned about it, is supportive and reassuring, and is actively experimenting with adjusting the medication to relieve the patient's distress.

Patients Who Refuse Medication

Some patients are extremely reluctant to take medication, even after considerable exploration of doubts and attempts at education. When the patient is adamant about refusing to take medication, the clinician may have little choice. Attempts to bully or threaten the patient into taking the medication are unwise and ineffective. The patient who under pressure reluctantly agrees to take medication will very likely have a poor record of compliance with the treatment regimen, while his resentment at having been "forced" to do so will seriously compromise the treatment alliance. Under such circumstances the clinician may be unable to assess the patient's response to medication, since the patient's statements about his reactions to the medication or about his compliance with the dosage schedule may not be reliable.

When a patient refuses medication and does not require hospitalization, it is best to continue treatment without medication and see if the patient can be persuaded to try the medication at a later date. Some patients (particularly patients with paranoid symptoms) are particularly concerned about their decision-making autonomy. They are frightened and suspicious of any proposal by the therapist. It is often useful to suggest that they take some time to think over the decision and that the matter can be deferred until some later meeting. Having established that they can successfully refuse medication, these suspicious patients may then be able to decide to give medication a try once a little time has passed. This process may be facilitated if the clinician suggests they try a dose or two before making a final decision. A patient who returns to a later meeting saying he is willing to try a course of medication can be counted on to be reasonably compliant and to discuss his reactions to the medication candidly. In these cases it is best to start the medication at very low doses and increase it very gradually. This gives the patient a chance to accustom himself to the effects of the medication gradually, avoiding potentially frightening rapid changes caused by full antipsychotic doses. With patients who persist in their opposition to medication, therapists may attempt to negotiate an agreement which specifies that the patient will try medication after a specified period of time if symptoms have not markedly improved.

Sometimes none of these tactics works. In these instances it may simply be necessary to wait, making it clear quietly that the patient's progress in treatment would be considerably greater with a course of medication. Some patients need to be treated entirely without medication, and such treatment often must be considerably more intensive and prolonged than treatment with medication combined with psychotherapy. Treatment without medication can occasionally be effective, but the likelihood is that treatment without medication will be, at best, substantially inferior.

It is unwise to present a patient with a forced choice of either a trial of antipsychotic medication or psychiatric hospitalization. Unless the patient is so severely ill that involuntary commitment to a psychiatric hospital is necessary, that ultimatum has little meaning. If the patient is in fact so seriously disturbed that involuntary hospitalization is indicated, the patient's willingness to take medication should be an irrelevant consideration. The time required for the onset of effective action of antipsychotic medication is sufficiently long so that starting a patient on medication is not in itself an effective alternative to hospitalization. Decisions about hospitalization and the need for medication should thus be kept carefully separate, and hospitalization should never be presented to the patient in a way which suggests that it is a punishment for noncompliance with any aspect of the treatment.

Outpatient treatment of psychotic patients is usually predicated, in part, on their compliance with a medication regimen. Nonetheless there are some quite disturbed patients who may be successfully treated on an outpatient basis even though they refuse to take antipsychotic medication. It is the dangerousness of the patient's condition and his overall capacity for collaboration in a treatment effort which must form the basis for a judgment about inpatient versus outpatient treatment, not simply the patient's compliance with the medication regimen.

When urging the patient who refuses medication to reconsider, the therapist must always attempt to convey his sense of the importance of medication in a tone of respectful concern. Once the point is clearly made, it is best to let the matter drop rather than to continuously nag a resistant patient. It rarely makes sense to predict dire consequences or to attempt to frighten a patient into compliance. Similarly, there is little to recommend telling the patient that treatment will continue only if he agrees to take antipsychotic medication. This may be an efficient way to get rid of a difficult and uncooperative patient, but its effect is usually destructive. The clinician who feels that he cannot cope with a patient who refuses to take medication can properly say so and assist the patient in finding a therapist who feels comfortable managing this particular therapeutic difficulty. This strategy is considerably different from telling a patient that he must take medication or the treatment will be abruptly terminated. In this instance the patient may choose to terminate the treatment and he may refuse further psychotherapeutic help or insist on consulting a clinician who is opposed to the use of antipsychotic medication. Worse, perhaps, a patient may agree to take medication to continue working with a therapist he knows and has come to trust, but he may be taking the medication intermittently or not at all. He may feel unable to discuss his noncompliance and misgivings openly in the treatment. The end result is that both the pharmacotherapy and the therapeutic alliance are compromised.

In general, the best way to deal with disagreements about major treatment issues like medication is to tolerate them with patience and to help make it possible for the patient to change his views and to make different decisions if events prove the clinician correct. If the patient refuses medication, his continued difficulty and distress may ultimately convince him of the need to accept antipsychotic medication as part of his treatment. This is most likely to happen if the clinician can accept a patient's refusal to take medication and can agree to treat the patient with the understanding that he views the treatment as compromised by the refusal.

> A 22-year-old auto repairman sought psychotherapeutic treatment at the urging of his family. He presented with the chief complaint, "I'm getting too nervous at work." The patient described a period of approximately one month during which he was increasingly anxious and uncomfortable. He complained of difficulty sleeping and the progressive withdrawal of friends and co-workers. In his initial clinical interview he was extremely anxious with pressured speech, looseness of associations, and bizarre delusions. He denied suicidal ideation and though he was in considerable distress he reported that he was able to function at work without attracting the concern or comment of his superiors.
>
> He flatly refused to take medication, stating that his problems were "not serious enough for powerful tranquilizers." He insisted on meeting the therapist once weekly, in part for "financial reasons," but also because he felt more frequent meetings, like taking medication, were an acknowledgment of the severity of his problems. The clinician agreed to meet with the patient on a weekly basis and the meetings were used to help define the patient's problems as one of severely high levels of anxiety and periods of confusion. During the patient's third visit the therapist mentioned that medication might help to reduce the levels of these symptoms and suggested that the patient think this over as a possible option to adopt in the future. During the fifth psychotherapeutic session the patient took the initiative in suggesting that he might be willing to try medication in small doses and for a brief period to see if it would be of any benefit. The remainder of that session was occupied with discussion of possible side effects. After taking an additional week to mull over this new information, the patient agreed to begin on modest doses of medication. He responded well and doses were gradually increased over subsequent weeks. By the twelfth visit the patient was on a moderate antipsychotic dose of medication with good clinical effect.

It is clear that in this instance the clinician ran some risk in permitting a long period of time to elapse before the patient began on antipsychotic medication. The patient's clinical condition might have deteriorated rapidly and resulted in some harm to the patient or others. Although the patient did not appear to be a danger to himself or others, the risk that his condition might worsen was greater once he refused to consider medication. On the other hand, the therapist felt that the patient's initial opposition to antipsychotic medication was so strong that any attempt to pressure him into taking the medication constituted a risk to the integrity of the treatment and thus a greater risk to his safety.

Some patients are resolute in their opposition to a trial of medication and their treatment may be compromised as a result. Psychotic symptoms may become chronic or may take many months to resolve under these circumstances. The patient's clinical condition may ultimately deteriorate and hospitalization may be necessary. In cases of this sort the therapist should bear with the patient and attempt to help him learn something from the experience. Eventually, the patient may be able to acknowledge that the deterioration of his condition may be connected to his refusal to take medication and he may be able to use the experience of hospitalization to reexamine his opposition to its use.

CHAPTER III

The Therapeutic Alliance

A GOOD WORKING ALLIANCE between patient and therapist is the single most important element in any psychotherapy. Without it little or nothing can be accomplished, and a poor working relationship usually results in disintegration of the treatment altogether. So central is this relationship that the course of a psychotherapeutic treatment can best be traced by following the evolution of the alliance between the therapist and patient. Because it is so crucial a matter, the therapeutic alliance must be a source of continuing concern and effort on the part of the clinician, no matter what disturbing or urgent events are unfolding in the treatment. Since the integrity of the treatment itself depends upon the quality of the therapeutic alliance, that relationship must take precedence over every other aspect of therapy, the sole exception to this axiom being an immediate and direct risk to the patient's life or safety (or to the life and safety of another person).

Building the Therapeutic Alliance

Building a satisfactory therapeutic alliance usually requires painstaking effort. Since therapists vary so widely in their personal styles, empathic skills, anxiety levels, and responses to patients and since patients vary so widely in their clinical presentations, no single approach to the problem can be prescribed. Each therapist must learn to use his or her experience and intuition to feel the way gradually toward the goal of an effective working collaboration.

A good therapeutic alliance does not require that patient and therapist be always on the best of terms. In fact, during the course of a successful treatment there may be on occasion considerable tension, anger, or disappointment openly expressed and discussed between them. So long as both retain a sense that they are working together toward a common goal, the relationship is usually strong enough to absorb these stresses and to survive difficult periods. How can the clinician know when the therapeutic alliance is strained and in difficulty? How does a sensitive clinician detect that the patient is losing faith in the treatment or has come to doubt the skill or commitment of his therapist?

There are no simple answers to these questions. The therapist must be continually alert and sensitive to this aspect of the treatment and take careful note of any comment, tone of voice, or behavior on the part of the patient which suggests difficulty in the working alliance. This does not mean that the therapist must comment on every such observation. Quite the contrary! Perhaps the most common technical error for beginning therapists is their tendency to comment so frequently about the patient's difficulty in the relationship that the patient feels nagged and harassed. This approach usually makes the patient conceal his misgivings to avoid having to dwell endlessly and unproductively on a troublesome subject. The therapist must be content with an occasional question or comment that makes note of a reasonably clear indication from the patient that he is doubtful or unhappy about his involvement in treatment. Even if the patient does not respond to this invitation to discuss his reservations, he will at least be reminded that the therapist is comfortable with and even interested in having them openly discussed.

Since psychotic patients are severely impaired, often suspicious of psychiatry, and frequently resistant to the treatment process, their capacity for alliance with a therapist is often initially tenuous and fragile. The patient may have been surprised by his illness and he may never have thought he had any psychological difficulty or need for treatment. He may feel totally unprepared for his encounter with a therapist and terrified of an unknown and unwanted treatment process. The patient who has suffered psychotic illness is often struggling desperately to regard his "breakdown" as an isolated episode in his life. He may therefore have an urgent and pressing need to think of himself as "normal" and to convince others that he is perfectly sane. Under these circumstances he is likely to regard the therapist as a dangerous adversary, a professional both able and determined to prove that he is handicapped and severely ill. The patient may feel condemned to participate in psychotherapy and may regard the treatment as a continuing humiliation. The patient who has come to see treatment as a stigmatizing badge of weakness rather than as a potential source of strength and growth certainly will be a reluctant collaborator in that process and will be intensely defensive and resistant to any exploratory effort.

The patient may give lip service to his investment in treatment, echoing a rationale imposed by others. An intense and only partially conscious fear of recurrent psychosis may provide the main motive behind the patient's continued willingness to participate, leading to a relationship in which the patient conceives of his role as one of needing to convince the therapist that he no longer has problems or needs treatment. The patient may fantasize that if he can convince the therapist that he is "normal and well," he can discontinue treatment without fear of relapse.

Given this constellation of fears, attitudes, and ambivalent feelings, the clinician should not be surprised that the early stages in the treatment of psychotic patients involve frequent and severe difficulties in the therapeutic alliance. These difficulties should be expected by the therapist who should regard them as treatment issues, rather than annoying and trouble-some obstacles. Attempts to frighten the patient into compli-ance with treatment by sternly lecturing him about the serious-ness of his illness are likely to stiffen resistance and emphasize the adversarial quality of the relationship. On the other hand, to reassure and support the patient's confidence in his "nor-mality" may undermine that patient's limited motivation to continue in treatment and is dishonest as well.

Most important, the therapist should remember that there is no quick or easy way to alter this state of affairs and establish an effective therapeutic alliance. Careful and patient efforts to uncover and explore the patient's resistance to treatment while educating him about his illness can lead to a gradual transfor-mation of the relationship. Since this process may take many months to accomplish, the clinician must avoid attempting to exact from the patient any early commitment to long-term com-pliance with either medication or psychotherapy. Even if the patient is sufficiently intimidated early in the treatment to agree to such a commitment, he is likely to resent the pressure and to feel that he has lost any control over the treatment. A genuine collaboration is essential to a treatment alliance that can sustain any exploratory work. Once the acute phase of treatment is completed, the treatment plans may have to be on a short-term but renewable basis with an understanding that the patient has serious reservations about treatment and will want to review his commitment frequently.

Not every sign of hesitancy and reluctance in the patient is related to problems in the therapeutic alliance, and the clinician should be careful not to draw premature conclusions. Unless the meaning of the patient's behavior is clear, it is best to wait and observe carefully, inviting exploration with open-ended questions rather than making direct interpretations. For exam-ple, a patient who is repeatedly late for therapy sessions may be indicating that he has serious reservations about all or part of the treatment. However, other explanations are possible. In the early stages of treatment psychotic patients may be late be-cause they are still disorganized and have difficulty functioning on a regular schedule. During the convalescent phase of illness many patients have difficulty tolerating a full hour and may come late in an unconscious effort to reduce the session to a more comfortable length. Other patients may be struggling with fantasies about the therapist's attitudes toward them. For example, they may be concerned that the therapist barely tolerates their presence, even in a shortened session.

Since there are so many possible explanations for this behavior, the clinician should approach it with patience and an open mind. The therapist may begin by simply noting that the patient is frequently late and inviting him to think about it in a collaborative way. The clinician should be mindful that even a carefully neutral observation of this sort may be heard by a patient as a criticism and a demand for punctuality. The patient may need to be reassured that the clinician will not be angry or critical if the tardiness continues, especially since careful exploration may clarify and ultimately resolve the difficulty. It may be necessary, for example, to have the patient meet for half-hour sessions until he is better able to tolerate a full session. In some instances the therapist may need to tolerate lateness for many months before the difficulty can be satisfactorily resolved.

Establishing a Therapeutic Atmosphere

The clinician who pays thoughtful attention to the tone and style of his work with psychotic patients can do a great deal to foster the development of a therapeutic atmosphere. Patients convalescing from an acute psychotic episode frequently express the hope that their therapist will "talk to them," and they complain bitterly if they are disappointed in this regard (although they may not complain directly to the therapist). The need to have a sensitive and responsive therapist is particularly strong in this group of insecure and easily alienated patients. It is not a wish for a chatty and talkative clinician; in fact, as treatment progresses most patients are increasingly uncomfortable with therapists who are continuously active, talkative, and directive. In the early stages of treatment psychotic patients are especially sensitive to rejection and fearful that they will be regarded as alien and repulsive. They want a therapist who can be a friendly and empathic professional, someone who listens attentively and is sincerely trying to respond and be helpful. They need a clinician who can appreciate that they have suffered a terrible experience and continue to be in great pain. Yet they also need reassurance that the therapist is not frightened or deeply distressed by their problems. They do not demand omniscience or perfection and they will usually forgive even serious errors if the clinician can admit them frankly.

The severity of their illness combined with their concerns about being stigmatized and alienated make patients who have suffered from psychosis particularly intolerant of therapists who appear to be withdrawn, emotionally distant, or who respond in stereotypical ways. Patients regard such therapists as hostile and unsympathetic—which indeed they are. By the same token, patients soon become uncomfortable if their therapist is unprofessionally friendly or blurs the boundaries of the professional role. While each therapist must find a unique balance between warmth, friendliness, and professional distance and discipline, the clinicians who work with psychotic patients should be willing to permit themselves to be defined more distinctly as persons than therapists who work with less troubled patients.

A psychotic patient may need to know basic facts about the therapist. These patients commonly look up their therapists's address and drive by his home to have a look. The therapist may be less frightening to them if they know, for example, whether he is married, has children, and where he trained. Information of this sort which is a matter of public record may be revealed to a curious patient if that appears to be helpful in making that patient comfortable in treatment. When patients raise these questions directly or indirectly, they usually deserve a direct and truthful response. In general, information which the clinician could comfortably share with an acquaintance can be revealed to psychotic patients without unduly complicating the treatment. Thus, for example, the psychotic patient who wants to know where his therapist will be going on vacation may be helped if he receives a straightforward answer. The patient may need a direct and specific answer so that he can comfortably ''locate'' his therapist psychologically during the break in treatment. On the other hand, details of the therapist's personal life—problems, tastes, political opinions and the like are best kept carefully private, since they can interfere with subsequent exploratory work.

Talking with Patients

The therapist should be scrupulously honest in all dealings with the patient. Few things are more destructive to the therapeutic alliance than deliberate deceptions, even when they appear to be in the best interests of the patients. However, the obligation to be truthful does not imply that the therapist must be brutally honest or must respond to any and every question. A tactful concern for the patient's sensitivities and anxieties is an equally important dimension in a mutually trusting relationship. On occasion this can present a problem for a therapist who is asked a difficult and direct question, a question he feels it would be unwise to answer candidly. First and foremost, the clinician must not lie. Evasion is permissible and possible but it may cause considerable anger and frustration in the patient. The traditional evasive cliche of psychotherapy, answering a question with a question (''I wonder why you asked me that?'') is a particularly infuriating and alienating mistake. When the motive or concern behind the question is genuinely of therapeutic importance, the therapist can respond by saying ''I will answer your question, but before I do so I'd like to know why you asked.'' Similarly, a silent refusal to respond to a troublesome question is also an unsatisfactory tactic. The therapist should always be mindful of the psychotic patient's sense that his psychosis stigmatizes and separates him from the rest of humanity. Such patients are apt to misinterpret or overreact to small signs of indifference or rebuff. A silent withdrawal on the part of the therapist may avoid a problematic question at the cost of provoking a painful withdrawal on the part of the patient, making it much less likely that the patient will feel free to raise potentially troublesome questions again.

Perhaps the best way to respond to overly personal or especially sensitive questions is for the therapist to take care to explain his behavior. While reassuring the patient that he has a right to ask any question, the therapist can explain that he will not respond because of a concern that a reply might interfere with later treatment. "I'd rather not answer that question because I think it would raise too many difficult issues and get us too far off the track."

Similarly, a patient's request for direction or guidance about what he should talk about can be met by saying "I don't know what it would be best to talk about today either, so I think it would be best for you to just try and tell me what's on your mind." This sort of response explains the therapist's refusal to be directive but avoids the tension generated by a therapist who simply sits in prolonged silence, waiting for the patient to begin to speak. While explanations of this sort can lead to an occasional discussion about the degree to which a therapist can and should control the content and atmosphere of the therapy, such a discussion can be of value and well worth the time it consumes. Unsophisticated patients often have a difficult time understanding why therapists behave as they do and they may disagree with the clinician's rationale for a particular response or reaction. For the most part, patients can accept a firm assertion that the therapist intends to stick to his judgment regarding matters of therapeutic technique and they are usually reassured by that firmness even while they maintain their disgruntlement. Although this way of responding to patients is occasionally time consuming and may create some friction in the therapy, it is of value because it acknowledges the therapist's evasions and passivity openly as technical necessities rather than leaving them unacknowledged and misinterpreted by the patient as rebuffs directed against him personally.

As in the above instances, it also may be important for the therapist to explain the basis for interpretations and interventions, particularly with patients suffering from paranoid symptoms. Explanations of this sort may help to reduce the anxiety of patients who are already fearful that "people know what I'm thinking." Identifying the verbal or nonverbal cues that form the basis for an interpretation or remark may help a frightened and confused patient to begin to understand how therapy works and how it might be useful. Although these explanations may lead to disagreements about the validity of the therapist's observations, the clinician can treat such disagreements as an inevitable part of the treatment process. Of course, the clinician should take care not to be drawn into elaborate discussion or debate about the basis for an interpretation.

The therapist's observations should be phrased in a way which permits disagreement and discussion on the part of the patient. The clinician should avoid even implying that the patient cannot think for himself or have a share in the control of the treatment. The convalescent phase of treatment requires that the therapist create an atmosphere of tolerance for disagreement and temporarily suspended judgment for both parties who can then safely and carefully explore questions of the patient's vulnerability to psychosis and the need for continued treatment.

The therapist should be careful to keep his language simple, understandable, and free from any trace of psychiatric jargon. Patients are often interested in jargon and will use it themselves and encourage the therapist to do the same. Many patients read psychiatric texts and articles and may know something about mental illness or at least give the appearance of knowing something. Patients are often concerned about antipsychotic medication and its effects and may seek to read about the subject on that account. Having the name of a specific medication they can look up gives them the opportunity to read about the conditions for which that medication is commonly prescribed. This identifies for them specific diagnostic entities and symptoms which they may read about to their growing distress, leading to questions within the treatment about diagnosis and requests for references to the psychiatric literature. The clinician must use his judgment about such requests, exploring what the patient has already read and whether further reading might make matters better or worse. In general, it is best to educate the patient within the treatment and the clinician should encourage the patient to explore these matters at length directly with the therapist. Patients frequently misunderstand the complexities of psychiatric diagnosis and may well confuse matters by reading outdated texts. The clinician can never assume that the patient understands the meaning or proper use of a technical term introduced into the treatment. It is essential that any discussion about treatment, symptoms, or diagnosis avoid technical terminology as much as possible and use commonplace words and descriptive phrases. Any technical term the patient employs should be defined or rephrased by the therapist in everyday language before it is used further.

A patient may ask the therapist directly for a diagnosis, and there is nothing remarkable about such a request. Patients commonly ask clinicians to provide them with a diagnosis and they have a right to expect a direct and honest answer. Clinicians who treat psychotic patients are often reluctant to respond directly, fearing that the patient will be unnecessarily alarmed. In the acute phase of treatment, the use of diagnostic labels often causes unnecessary distress and complicates an already difficult and turbulent situation. During this period any questions about the patient's diagnosis are best deferred until some stability has been achieved. Such a delay may be necessary in any case, since the clinician may be unable to make a definite diagnosis until some time has elapsed in the treatment. When the patient raises the question again later, a frank response is best.

Some patients are satisfied with a diagnosis of "psychotic disorder." However, most patients require more specific diagnostic information. Patients with bipolar disorders need to be told this diagnosis and educated about its implications. "Schizophreniform disorder" is a term which requires explanation for most patients. Patients with schizophrenic disorders may ask directly about their diagnosis and should be given an honest response. However, the term "schizophrenia" is often particularly frightening for patients and their families and considerable explanation and reassurance may be necessary once patients have been told this diagnosis.

Limits and Boundaries

The therapist's openness and candor needs to be balanced by careful attention to professional distance and discipline. It is important to have regular, scheduled hours to meet with patients and the sessions should begin and end at the scheduled times. Therapists who are genuinely friendly people and who tend to like their patients have a distinct advantage in their work, provided they are careful not to let this friendliness deteriorate into familiarity and casual intimacy. Within the framework of regularly scheduled interviews there is considerable room for variation as to a therapist's attire, forms of address employed, and the degree of formality in his or her behavior. The therapist's adherence to the defined goals of the relationship permits exploration of a wide variety of styles and nuances in establishing relationships with patients. However, it is essential that the clinician be predictable and consistent in his approach and style.

The clinician must have clearly in mind the boundaries required for psychotherapeutic effectiveness and must be willing to set firm limits when necessary. If a patient needs more time with the therapist, extra hours can be scheduled. The extra sessions should be conducted in the clinician's office during regular working hours. Any development so urgent it cannot wait until the next day is properly considered an emergency and should be evaluated in an emergency room setting. Physical contact between patient and therapist should be limited to the customary occasional handshake. Any more elaborate physical contact (such as hugs or pats) is likely to be experienced by the patient as seductive and may well cause serious difficulty.

The clinician can be flexible about some limits, expressing preferences clearly but not insisting on immediate compliance. For example, patients may need reminding that they are expected to sit in a chair, rather than on the floor or that it is customary to take off one's overcoat or keep on one's socks. On the other hand, limits must be set firmly and enforced on any behavior which makes effective treatment very difficult or impossible. For example, a patient should be told that it is not permissible to light up a marijuana cigarette during a session and that doing so will bring the session to an immediate end. Similarly, patients should be informed that treatment cannot be conducted if they arrive under the influence of drugs or alcohol.

Patients should gradually be taught to respect the clinician's privacy. Telephone calls to the clinician after business hours should be made through an answering service or office, not directly, affording the clinician some privacy and some control over when the call is returned. In addition, this arrangement gives the clinician a telephone number which can be useful if a troubled and uncooperative patient must be located in an emergency. Psychotherapy with psychotic patients cannot be conducted on the telephone. Except for the acute phase of treatment, telephone conversations should be limited to the exchange of important messages about scheduling of sessions and urgent matters should be dealt with by extra sessions as required, not explored on the telephone.

Dealing with Major Disagreements

Therapists often have difficulty tolerating the prolonged period of strained relationship and tenuous collaboration required in the early stages of treatment. The process of encouraging patients to be open and candid about their reservations and disagreements frequently leads to a period in which patient and therapist have agreed to tolerate major differences between them about such fundamental matters as the need for treatment and the patient's vulnerability to recurrent psychosis. Patients who are prone to psychosis are often capable of stoutly asserting convictions that are not only irrational but provocative and cheerfully indifferent to obvious conflicting evidence.

The therapist may often be tempted to tease or confront the patient in an effort to make him "face the truth." Acting on these impulses is usually counterproductive, either alienating the patient or leading to arguments with a subsequent deterioration of the therapeutic relationship. Provocative statements on the part of the patient must be dealt with courteously and the clinician should always take them seriously and respond accordingly.

On the other hand, it is useful and necessary for therapists to register disagreement with unreasonable or unlikely assertions and to make it clear that open disagreement with the patient is not only tolerable but probably an inevitable part of the treatment process. The possibility of error must be acknowledged by the therapist and the patient should be invited to suspend judgment while both examine the evidence and attempt to clarify any point in contention. The therapist, being willing to admit error, may provide an important role model for the patient. If the therapist can comfortably acknowledge a possible mistake, the patient may then be able to change his views without feeling humiliated or defeated. Obviously, when the therapist has made a clear error in judgment or misunderstood a matter of importance, a frank, simple, and prompt admission of the fact is an absolute necessity.

While disagreements, even about fundamental issues, are tolerable and to some extent inevitable in the early phases of treatment, arguments between the patient and therapist are not. It is rarely helpful to confront the patient's denial aggressively, citing abundant evidence like a prosecuting attorney. This point seems obvious and is generally understood intuitively by most therapists. It is therefore surprising how frequently patients recovering from psychosis are regarded as an exception to this basic tenet of psychotherapy. There is something about the massive denial of so severe an illness and the risk of premature termination of treatment and subsequent relapse into psychosis that may prompt therapists to react with a destructive and aggressive urgency. The therapist should calmly and patiently disagree with a patient when necessary, awaiting the moment when a more direct challenge to the patient and some degree of disciplined confrontation may be useful. These direct challenges must be controlled with great care. They should be reserved for such fundamental issues as the need for continued treatment, discontinuing medication, or acknowledging vulnerability to recurrent psychosis. A carefully timed and disciplined challenge to the patient may be a spur to engagement in the treatment. It may make it possible for the patient to acknowledge the seriousness of his difficulties and to form the beginning of an effective working alliance. These challenges should occur only when it is clear that a patient has directly raised the issue and insists that it be addressed.

A 24-year-old man was referred for outpatient treatment after a one-month hospital stay for severe psychotic illness precipitated by cocaine abuse. At the time of his outpatient referral he was free of overt psychotic symptoms and was mildly depressed. He was maintained on moderate doses of antipsychotic medication. A cooperative patient who presented with a bland, polite facade, he freely acknowledged that his cocaine use had been excessive. He felt that by avoiding drugs in the future he could eliminate any risk of recurrent psychosis. Although he insisted that his life was otherwise free of problems, he gradually and somewhat reluctantly described a lonely and isolated life which centered entirely around his work and his recreational drug use. Feeling lost and adrift after graduating from college, he held several unrewarding jobs and finally returned to work as a salesclerk in his college town. His college friends had moved on and all of his attention and social life was centered on his job. Most of his acquaintances were coworkers and it was with them that he took drugs. His family lived in a distant city and he saw them infrequently.

While conceding, in a detached way, that his life presented some problems, he described them as comparatively minor and in no way related to his illness. One month after beginning his twice weekly psychotherapy sessions and after receiving a bill for the first month of treatment, he began a session with an angry assertion of his resentment at the implication that he needed continued treatment—the first sign of genuine emotion he had shown since his treatment began. He reiterated that his difficulties were solely the result of his drug abuse and that he had recovered and was therefore perfectly normal and at no risk whatever for recurrent psychosis. The therapist quietly registered his disagreement, saying he was not yet convinced the patient had fully recovered and was free of any vulnerability to relapse. The patient responded with considerable annoyance, insisting that the therapist explain and justify his views. The clinician insisted that his convalescence was still incomplete and quietly reminded him of the difficulties he had described in previous hours. He suggested that the patient's loneliness and isolation were the major factors which led to his drug use and that they continued to be problems which might tempt him to again seek solace in drugs.

Although he continued to be angry, the patient responded with some interest, repeatedly insisting that the therapist elaborate and explain his statements. The tone of the discussion remained tense and confrontational throughout the hour. Nevertheless, the patient remained an interested and active participant in the process, creating for the first time a sense of genuine give and take between himself and the clinician.

None of the disagreements between therapist and patient were resolved during this session. However, during the next hour the patient was considerably more relaxed and able to speak more freely. He had been able to think over the content of the previous session and was willing to acknowledge that he had been painfully unhappy during the year prior to his psychotic episode and that his drug use was prompted by an attempt to seek relief from his distress. This proved to be the beginning of a productive psychotherapy.

Faced with a patient who is resistant and argumentative, it is easy for the clinician to underestimate the patient's investment in the therapeutic relationship, and the therapist may be tempted to assume that the patient is wholly opposed to treatment. In fact, these patients are often highly ambivalent about treatment and they may be counting on the therapist to tolerate their disagreement and denial. The clinician who can stand his ground and maintain a disciplined control over confrontations can sometimes overcome much of the patient's resistance and establish a strong therapeutic alliance, as in the following example.

A 27-year-old college graduate was referred for outpatient psychotherapy after a two month hospital stay for a manic psychosis. His psychotic symptoms were effectively controlled with a combination of neuroleptic medication and lithium. Upon discharge from the hospital he continued to manifest a mildly grandiose personality style in which a global denial of illness was combined with a confident and condescending attitude in his dealings with the therapist. From the outset the clinician adopted a tactic of openly and firmly disagreeing with the most clearly unreasonable and overconfident assertions of the patient. This occasionally led to lively disagreements with the patient about his psychotic illness and previous serious difficulties in work and social spheres. These disagreements usually ended in tense but polite stalemate.

This patient was an intelligent man who enjoyed the challenge of debate. At his highest level of premorbid functioning he had been actively involved in intellectual pursuits that involved frequent stimulating debates. Knowing this, the therapist repeatedly pointed out that disagreements within the therapy should be settled on the basis on an examination of the evidence, not by sweeping global assertions or appeals to authority. This challenge eventually appealed to the patient and although it often proved particularly difficult and painful to him, he was able to use the resulting "debates" to learn about himself. He was gradually able to modify his views and to acknowledge that he had been struggling with serious difficulties during the several years prior to his psychotic illness. After several months the "debates" gradually subsided and were replaced by lively and animated discussions. Although he continued to be inclined to argue and disagree, he began to realize this was his characteristic way of approaching issues and he was able to use his considerable wit and intelligence to soften this trait so that it no longer interfered with the therapeutic alliance. The patient was able to make considerable therapeutic use of the insight generated by these discussions.

However, at times there is no real opportunity for constructive confrontation and the therapist must simply express his views and wait. This strategy is often uncomfortable for the therapist, but it bears far richer rewards than a series of stormy and unproductive confrontations.

A college student was first hospitalized briefly at the age of 21 for a psychotic episode precipitated by hallucinogenic drug use. Although he was cooperative in the hospital he refused treatment after discharge, insisting that his recovery was complete and that his illness was caused solely by drug use. He returned to school and functioned reasonably well. Six months after graduation from college, he was again hospitalized for two weeks for a recurrence of psychotic symptoms. He denied using hallucinogenic drugs at any time during the months prior to this second episode. The hospital staff recommended a longer period of inpatient treatment, but the patient insisted on discharge after a few weeks. He reluctantly agreed to continue treatment and was referred to an outpatient therapist. He was discharged from the hospital on a moderate dose of antipsychotic medication.

Although he gradually became involved in his outpatient therapy, he continued to insist that medication was unnecessary and he gradually discontinued it, despite his therapist's firm recommendation to the contrary. Approximately ten weeks after discontinuing the medication, he was again hospitalized for a recurrence of psychotic symptoms. During the three subsequent years of his treatment his medication compliance remained excellent. The resulting stability permitted the focus of treatment to shift to his social concerns and developmental problems. During the last year of treatment medication was reduced and finally discontinued after the patient successfully completed several months in graduate school.

Although this patient required hospitalization for psychotic symptoms on three separate occasions, he was able to make use of these experiences on each occasion to learn something about the nature of his illness and its treatment. The attempts of his therapist to help him understand these matters while tolerating disagreement made it possible for the patient to acknowledge gradually the degree of his overall vulnerability to psychosis. The result was not merely good medication compliance, but a stable, trusting therapeutic alliance which permitted psychotherapy to go forward.

Once an effective working relationship has been established, the treatment can change in focus and become more productive. Of course, the working alliance requires continuing attention and nurturance. The psychotic patient, who begins treatment reluctantly, may gradually come to be a willing and constructive participant in the treatment process. It is only as this shift develops and progresses that the work of treatment can shift from supportive, rehabilitative, and prophylactic goals to a more ambitious exploration of developmental difficulties and conflicts.

CHAPTER IV

Convalescence

ANY CLINICIAN who imagines that antipsychotic medications provide a fully effective treatment for acute psychosis need only observe patients in the early stages of their convalescence to appreciate both the value and limitations of these agents. Antipsychotic medication is clearly an enormous asset in the treatment of acute psychosis. Its power to control and suppress symptoms has made it the cornerstone of contemporary treatment of psychotic illness. Despite its value, however, it is far from a complete treatment, a fact which is particularly evident during convalescence from the acute episode. Once acute symptoms have been controlled the patient enters a period of convalescence, which can vary greatly in its duration and clinical presentation. For most patients the convalescent period lasts from a few months to a year after the acute psychotic episode. Typically, patients improve throughout the course of convalescence, although the rate of improvement is uneven and tends to slow as the patient approaches premorbid levels of function.

It is difficult to predict which patients will have a slow or troubled convalescence and which will progress rapidly following the acute psychotic episode. However, the speed of improvement in convalescence often is roughly a mirror image of the speed at which the decompensation occurred. Thus, patients whose acute psychotic state developed rapidly and interrupted a relatively high level of premorbid functioning appear more likely to have a comparatively rapid convalescence with successful early return to their premorbid state. Patients whose illness developed insidiously or who have had multiple previous psychotic episodes appear more likely to suffer a prolonged and difficult convalescence. To some extent, patients who respond well to antipsychotic medication appear to experience a smoother convalescence. A variety of personal and individual factors also shape the patient's convalescence in important ways. Personal, intellectual, family, and financial resources can exercise an important influence on the duration and outcome of convalescence, since each of these factors can influence the motivation and capacity of both patient and family to comply with treatment.

Residual Symptoms

For most patients, florid psychotic symptoms such as disorganization, delusions, and hallucinations have been suppressed nearly completely by antipsychotic medication by the end of the acute phase of illness. However, convalescence from psychosis is almost invariably complicated by residual symptoms which compromise function and alter personality in comparison to the patient's premorbid state. Residual thought disorder is usually mild and subtle, appearing most prominently when the patient is stressed or required to express some complex idea. Delusional ideas are usually absent or they are held with less conviction during convalescence and may be elicited only on direct questioning. Convalescing patients are quite often concrete in their thinking and speech, approaching tasks with a solemn literal-mindedness. Their capacity for sustained concentration is usually impaired and a short attention span is common even when the patient is engaging in pleasant activities.

A combination of these deficits usually produces significant impairment in cognitive and social functioning which, while not blatant, is readily apparent when the patient is examined at all closely. In particular, higher level intellectual function is often significantly impaired in comparison with premorbid abilities. Constriction of affect is also common. Patients in the convalescent phase of their illness are typically cautious and controlled, presenting a bland and neutral facade. They usually behave as if they are extremely frightened of any degree of emotional arousal and they protect themselves against a possible "loss of control" by suppressing all but the most muted of their feelings.

Medication Side Effects

When neuroleptic medication is used in full antipsychotic doses the incidence of undesirable side effects is high. Patients often confuse side effects with allergies, and the clinician should make the distinction clear. Sedation is perhaps the most common problem and patients often complain of difficulties in staying awake. As psychotic agitation decreases, the sedative effects of the medication may become more prominent. Patients may sleep long hours and are often heavy-lidded and drowsy much of the day. Although they may be able to maintain an alert awareness for limited periods of time (for example during a psychotherapy session), the clinician should be careful not to assume that the drowsiness the patient reports is therefore of psychological origin. Although tolerance to this side effect often develops with the passage of time, gradual reduction of the dosage of medication to maintenance levels is often necessary before this symptom improves. A change to a less sedating neuroleptic may be indicated if sedation continues to pose problems at maintenance dosage levels.

Other common side effects of neuroleptic drugs include dry

mouth, blurred vision, constipation, and postural hypoten-
sion. These symptoms are usually worse during the initial
stages of treatment and tend to improve gradually as tolerance
develops and as the dosage of medication is reduced to maintenance levels. Heat intolerance and photosensitivity reactions to
exposure to sunlight are less common. Nevertheless, patients
should be advised to use a sun-screen preparation and avoid
excessive heat during the summer months.

Extrapyramidal side effects occur frequently and can be
quite uncomfortable. A parkinsonian syndrome may develop
which can include akinesia, rigidity, and tremor. Akinesia involves a generalized decrease in voluntary movement with an
associated wooden, mask-like lack of facial expression. "Cog-
wheel" rigidity and resting tremor which disappears with
movement are also characteristic of this syndrome. Akathisia, a
motor restlessness in which the patient has great difficulty sit-
ting still and experiences a nearly constant involuntary urge to
move, is another delayed-onset neurological side effect often
experienced by patients on antipsychotic drugs. Dystonic reactions may also occur, typically shortly after the initiation of
antipsychotic drug therapy and most frequently in adolescents.
They include facial grimacing, torticollis, and oculogyric crisis.
Dystonic reactions are especially frightening to both patients
and families and therefore advance discussion of this possible
side effect is essential.

Extrapyramidal side effects can be decreased and controlled
to some degree by adding an antiparkinson medication such
as trihexyphenidyl (Artane) or benztropine (Cogentin) to the
treatment regimen. These agents are somewhat less helpful in
the control of akathisia. Dystonic reactions are readily controlled by a variety of agents including antiparkinson and anti-
histaminic agents.

Patients on neuroleptic medication may gain weight, sometimes fairly rapidly. Increasing weight during the convalescent
period is sometimes a serious problem, so much so that some
patients are reluctant to comply with the medication regimen.
Women, in particular, may find the change in their appearance

unacceptable. Dieting may help, but patients often find that weight loss is particularly difficult.

Other rare side effects include urinary retention, the exacerbation of glaucoma, breast swelling, and lactation. Thioridazine may cause inhibition of ejaculation and in doses above 800 mg per day may cause pigmentary retinopathy. Neuroleptic drugs may cause infrequent toxic hematologic or hepatic reactions. These toxic reactions usually occur during the first months of treatment. Frequent blood tests are not particularly useful in monitoring patients for these conditions, but the patient should be observed carefully for any clinical signs or symptoms suggesting toxicity, e.g., persistent infection.

Lithium, particularly in higher therapeutic dosages can cause a wide variety of side effects. Most common is a tremor which the patient may find quite unpleasant. The tremor is variable in intensity and is often worse when the patient is anxious or under stress. Gastrointestinal symptoms such as nausea, vomiting, and diarrhea may also occur. Lithium usually causes increased thirst and increased urine volume and in some patients the increase is enough to disturb sleep and interfere with social functioning. On rare occasion a lithium-induced nephrogenic diabetes insipidus may occur. Lithium occasionally causes a troubling acne and hair loss. Because of the possibility of lithium-related abnormalities in thyroid and kidney function, patients should have a physical examination and appropriate laboratory tests done yearly. The use of lithium during pregnancy is associated with an increased incidence of fetal anomalies, and patients should be advised of this risk.

Tardive Dyskinesia

Tardive dyskinesia is a serious complication of treatment with neuroleptic medication. It usually occurs after prolonged treatment with these agents and it is more common in women and in older patients. The dyskinesia consists of abnormal movements of the mouth, face, jaw, and tongue. Sometimes movements of the extremities and trunk are involved as well. These symptoms may worsen initially when the drug is discontinued, although they may ultimately improve and in over one-third of cases will disappear altogether after the drug is stopped. However, for the remaining majority of patients the condition is permanent, though it is usually not disabling.

An essential component of the therapist's efforts to educate the patient is a review of the risks associated with extended use of neuroleptic medication. Since the acute phase of psychosis is often tense or turbulent, a full discussion of risks may be deferred until convalescence. Tardive dyskinesia is extremely rare during the first three months of treatment, so the clinician can safely delay discussion of this crucial subject until the patient is well over the acute phase of illness. Because tardive dyskinesia is such a serious potential complication, the clinician should take care to document in his records that informed consent was obtained from the patient and, where appropriate, from family members as well. However, most clinicians do not insist on written consent.

In addition to describing the disorder, the clinician should consider including the following points in his discussion: (1) It is not possible to predict how likely it is that any given patient will develop tardive dyskinesia; (2) There is no effective way to prevent tardive dyskinesia from occuring—anyone taking the medication is at risk; (3) Treatment of psychosis without neuroleptic medication is certainly less effective in controlling psychotic symptoms and preventing relapse; (4) The medication is not an absolute protection against relapse; and (5) The clinician should make it clear that he is firmly convinced that the benefits of continued treatment with antipsychotic medication far outweigh the risks at this stage of the patient's treatment. For a fuller review of this topic, the reader is referred to the excellent discussion in Jeste and Wyatt (1982).

Postpsychotic Apathy and Depression

Some degree of inertia and apathetic social withdrawal appear to be a nearly universal aspect of convalescence from psychotic

Passivity or with-drawal

illness. Whether this passivity and withdrawal are the result of medication effect, demoralization, and/or depression or represent a separate dimension of psychotic illness is not at all clear. In any case, the patient appears to have only a very limited control over this apathetic state and cannot be expected to "snap out of it." In addition, some patients develop a clear depressive syndrome which complicates the convalescent period. Manic patients may gradually slip into a depressive phase of their illness. However, no matter what the nature of the initial psychotic episode, some degree of apathy and passive withdrawal is nearly always present. When depressive symptoms are prominent, appropriate treatment with antidepressant medication can sometimes be helpful, although in this complex clinical picture, differentiating symptoms of melancholia is often difficult.

Early Reactions to the Psychotic Episode

In addition to residual psychotic symptoms and medication side effects, the convalescing patient is struggling with his first sustained opportunity to think about and react to the fact that he has suffered a major psychiatric illness. Although patients vary greatly in their capacity to cope with the fact that they have suffered a psychotic illness, most are struggling, openly or covertly, to control a terrified sense of having suffered an alienating and stigmatizing disorder. Coping with a fear of relapse into psychosis or of a future blighted by episodes of recurrent psychosis are central concerns dominating the convalescent period, although patients may be reluctant to talk about these fears in detail and may struggle to maintain an optimistic attitude. Similarly, a profound sense of shame at having been "insane" may be a private preoccupation of patients entering convalescence.

Patients who have had a number of psychotic episodes may be more demoralized than fearful or ashamed and may begin convalescence with a pessimistic sense that they are doomed to repeated episodes. They may be struggling with a sense of hopelessness which leads them to feel there is little point in attempting to lead a normal existence. Often they are child-like and dependent in their dealings with family members and therapist. Any clinician attempting to treat such patients should be capable of feeling and conveying some sense of reasonable therapeutic optimism. Patients need to feel that progress is still possible, despite limitations and setbacks. Each patient must have some confidence that the therapist believes his condition can be improved and that he can achieve better control of his life.

Once acute psychotic symptoms have subsided, both the patient and family may be alarmed and confused by the changes in the patient early in the convalescent period. Quite often the convalescing patient attributes all of his difficulties to the medication, complaining bitterly about real, imagined, or exaggerated side effects. Family members also may insist that difficulties with the medication are the only remaining problems and that the patient is otherwise rapidly returning to normal. This conviction may make it difficult to persuade them that continuing treatment with medication is essential to protect the patient against possible relapse.

Common Difficulties in Distinguishing Convalescent Symptoms

Sorting out the many possible symptoms, syndromes, medication side effects, and psychological reactions to psychotic illness can be an especially difficult challenge for the clinician. For example, akinesia needs to be differentiated from apathy and social withdrawal. These in turn can be confused with a depressive syndrome. Akathisia may be misinterpreted as agitation, anxiety, or an exacerbation of psychosis. Dystonia may be confused with hysteria. Emotional constriction needs to be distinguished from parkinsonian inhibition of expressiveness. Demoralization in response to psychotic illness can be confused with melancholia. In light of these complexities, the clinician should be alert to the likelihood of error in sorting out these symptoms and should be prepared to explore alternative hypotheses. Clinicians who are not psychiatrists may need to rely on a colleague who is in charge of medication to assess the patient for side effects and to help the therapist differentiate these symptoms and assist in the education of the patient and family about these matters.

The Transition from Hospital to Outpatient Treatment

For patients who are treated in the hospital during the period of acute psychosis, the transition from hospital to outpatient treatment is typically stressful and difficult. The anxiety associated with leaving the protected hospital setting usually causes some increase in the patient's symptoms. The anxiety of family members is also increased and the patient's return home is often awkward and tense for all concerned. The quality and duration of hospital treatment may have an important bearing on the patient's state when beginning outpatient treatment. A patient who is treated on a short-term basis in a hospital setting may be discharged in the earliest stages of convalescence with major residual symptoms, severe medication side effects, and a minimum of education about his illness. Bewildered by the hospital experience, these patients often come to outpatient treatment with major misconceptions about the treatment process and are likely to have a poor record of treatment compliance at a time when the risk of relapse is greatest. In such circumstances, the clinician should begin treatment while the patient is still in the hospital and meet frequently with both the patient and family during the period of hospitalization, as well as in the weeks after discharge, until all are securely engaged in treatment.

Patients in active and comprehensive hospital treatment programs may enter and negotiate the more difficult early phases of convalescence within the hospital setting and become outpatients in more stable condition and better educated about their illness than those discharged after the first signs of improvement. Some hospital programs work intensively on re-socializing and supporting patients while educating both the patient and family about psychotic illness and its treatment. In these instances patients may even have had an opportunity to learn something about outpatient treatment before referral to the outpatient clinician.

In any case, the outpatient clinician cannot assume that the patient has a realistic grasp of his illness, its treatment, or the reason for outpatient referral. Patient and family may initially give lip service to what they have been told by hospital personnel, but in-depth inquiry may soon reveal a good deal of confusion and ambivalence about outpatient treatment. The clinician is well advised to begin with a complete history obtained from the patient and family members which includes their report of the treatment received up to that point. The degree of their understanding, distortion, and misperception about the illness and treatment defines the state of their knowledge for the clinician and indicates where initial work must begin.

Patients whose psychotic episodes have been managed entirely on an outpatient basis may have a smoother and briefer convalescence, usually because such patients had better premorbid function and family resources to begin with. In addition, by avoiding psychiatric hospitalization the patient avoids some of the regressive and stigmatizing effects of inpatient treatment. However, avoiding inpatient treatment also makes it easier for the patient and his family to deny the seriousness of the psychotic episode. As a result they may minimize the need for ongoing prophylactic treatment. In such instances, it is important for the therapist to begin educational efforts during the acute phase of illness and to continue them on a fairly intensive basis during the early stages of the patient's convalescence.

Initial Attitudes Toward Outpatient Treatment

Psychotic outpatients usually come to treatment with attitudes and experiences markedly different from those of neurotic pa-

. tients. The neurotic patient who comes voluntarily to outpatient treatment generally has had considerable time to think about his disorder before seeking help. He may have done some reading about psychotherapy or talked about his difficulty with friends. After a period of rationalization, denial, or attempts at solving his difficulty, the neurotic patient gradually accepts the idea that he may need professional assistance.

In contrast, first-break psychotic patients are thrust abruptly into treatment with little or no preparation. The illness is usually a shocking surprise to those who regarded themselves as in no way ill prior to the onset of psychosis. The psychotic patient is frequently uninformed about psychotherapy and often harbors misconceptions about treatment which include many naive stereotypes and prejudices. These patients are usually terrified, bewildered, and resentful of what they regard as a sudden insistence on the part of family members and hospital personnel that they are in need of intensive and prolonged psychotherapy. The psychotic patient whose illness developed insidiously over a long period of time may arrive at outpatient treatment with great difficulty in understanding how the labeled illness differs from his conception of ''normality.''

Consequently, patients with psychotic disorders often need time to work on these ''preparatory issues'' during the convalescent phase of their illness. The clinician is therefore likely to encounter a patient undergoing a wide variety of reactions to the realization that he has suffered a major psychiatric illness and to the problems of treatment with both medication and psychotherapy. Most patients are embarrassed as they recall details of their bizarre behavior. They may be mortified at the prospect of meeting with friends or colleagues who saw them during the period of acute psychosis. A patient may fear that outpatient therapy will involve a humiliating, prolonged, and painful exploration of these events in order to brand him a ''mental case.''

The therapist should be prepared for major misconceptions about treatment, no matter how the patient arrives at outpatient therapy. For example, some convalescing patients believe that outpatient treatment should involve a few visits for a month or so to "wind things up." Others imagine that infrequent visits to an outpatient clinician for periodic "check-ups" are all that is required. Such notions are often an expression of the wish that the psychotic episode be transient and forgotten as soon as possible. Other patients understand that a longer period of outpatient treatment is required. However, they may have little sense of what the content of such treatment is likely to involve and they may be very apprehensive about the therapist's intentions. They may regard outpatient referral as punishment for misbehavior or as a form of custodial control. The patient may feel like a criminal who is now on carefully supervised parole, with the therapist allied with family members to keep the patient under surveillance.

Family members may also feel frightened and guilty at the prospect of outpatient treatment. They may feel relieved that they have been spared being saddled with the blame for the psychotic episode during the period of acute crisis. However, now that matters are under control, family members may fear that the purpose of continuing treatment is to investigate matters and assign blame. Parents often harbor considerable guilt about earlier marital or family difficulties. Their child's illness may seem to them the confirmation of their worst fears about themselves and they may be dreading what they regard as inevitable condemnation by a professional expert. These concerns may be intensified by the fact that family members may have behaved badly during the early stages of the patient's psychotic illness. Because they failed to recognize the seriousness of the developing psychosis, family members often feel blameworthy and guilty about having initially reacted sternly, angrily, unsympathetically, or indifferently. Patients may be aware of their parents' fears and may feel an urgent need to protect them from any further distress. Patients often also feel considerable guilt and regret about the pain they have caused family members during their illness and may fear that further pain will be inflicted on family members by treatment focusing on "parental mistakes."

No matter how healthy or troubled the family was before the onset of the patient's psychotic illness, the therapist can expect that the family will not be at its best during the patient's convalescence. The combination of grief, anxiety, resentment, and guilt that family members invariably experience when a child or sibling has suffered a psychotic illness usually leaves them exhausted, defensive, and frightened. Given these fears and tensions, outpatient treatment should not begin with an exploration of family problems. The clinician should begin by educating the patient and family about treatment, correcting misconceptions, and giving support and reassurance sufficient to reduce anxiety and guilt. Early in the treatment it is also important to convey to both patient and family basic information about the process of convalescence from psychotic illness. Even a fearful and defensive family may be able to accept guidance and advice during the early stages of convalescence if the clinician makes it clear that patients recovering from psychotic illness have unique problems which require expert assistance. The family should be helped to understand that the clinician's interventions do not imply criticism or blame, but rather are an attempt to help the family cope with a special situation which is unlike any encountered in ordinary experience.

Structuring the Convalescent Environment

The convalescent environment must be structured carefully. High school students should return to classes as soon as possible. A telephone call to the school guidance counselor may help to smooth the patient's return. The clinician should emphasize the fact that the patient's intellectual functioning is likely to be below par for at least several months, perhaps longer. A reduced course load and discussions with teachers about the problems of convalescence from psychotic illness may make it possible for the patient to have the benefits of attending school regularly without suffering unnecessary additional humiliation and defeat.

Patients are often very apprehensive about returning to school. The clinician can be of considerable help by discussing in detail with the patient how he might handle questions about his illness, particularly about any psychotic behavior which others might have observed at school. Patients are often frightened of being teased by their fellow students. This is less a problem for middle and upper class high school students than in lower social class settings where psychotic illness is usually more stigmatizing. In most instances classmates are awkward in dealing with the returning patient and are afraid of him and for him. As a result they are usually uncertain about how to approach him or what to say. Much depends on the patient's capacity to handle inquiries and awkward situations calmly and directly. Knowing that fellow students may be uncertain about approaching him, the patient can take the initiative in putting classmates at ease. The clinician's advice must be tailored to the individual situation, but in general it is wise for the patient to avoid going into detail about his illness with friends and classmates. He should be reassured that he has a right to privacy and that he can politely refuse to discuss sensitive matters. Discussion in advance about these matters with the patient is essential.

The combination of residual symptoms and medication side effects may make it impossible for the patient to return to a high school athletic team, although a discussion with the team coach can at times make it possible for the patient to participate in athletics on a limited basis. In most instances the patient will find it easier simply to skip participation in athletics for a season or so.

College students present more difficult problems. The intellectual demands of college are considerably greater than those of high school and poor academic performance in college can have a major impact on subsequent career opportunities. Most college students live away and therefore lack the support, encouragement, and structure that can be provided through living at home. Difficulties with abstraction and concentration combined with a lack of structure in most college settings usually make a rapid return to college inadvisable during convalescence. When patients return to college prematurely the academic difficulties they suffer can lead to demoralization and increased risk of relapse. The clinician should be alert to pressures from family members who may be pushing the patient to return to college rapidly for financial or status reasons. Intervention by the therapist is often crucial in combating these additional family pressures. In addition, therapists should take care that their own values do not distort their judgment. As educated people, clinicians in general favor education and may unconsciously pressure the patient, along with the family, into a premature resumption of academic work.

With rare exceptions, it is probably best that the college student remain at home for one or two semesters during convalescence, depending on the time of his illness, his school schedule, and the rate of his recovery. In a few instances the home environment is so difficult or unpleasant that other possibilities must be explored. Even in such instances an early return to school is contraindicated. Placement in a halfway house, living with friends or relatives, or sharing an apartment with peers may be useful in helping to tide the patient over the convalescent period.

Although it is usually advisable for college students to delay returning to school, it is important that they not be idle. Some structured employment is especially helpful in keeping patients active and in speeding the return of confidence. The contact with other people and sense of accomplishment provided by the experience of regular employment helps in preparation for resumption of college work. A job that does not demand high levels of intellectual functioning and that is reasonably structured and predictable is most likely to meet the needs of the convalescing college student. For example, work as a salesclerk, waiter, industrial lab technician, and the like are the sorts of jobs commonly available for college age patients: jobs which do not make excessive demands. The patient can also be advised to take night courses at a local college as a way of testing academic readiness and preparing the return to school.

Patients who were employed fulltime when their illness began should return to work as soon as possible. Here the clinician must use his judgment based on the patient's resources, rate of recovery, and the nature of the work involved. In some instances intervention with employers may be useful, particularly if the patient was overtly psychotic while at work. The employer and the patient's coworkers may need reassurance that the patient has recovered and guidance on how to deal with him or her. The clinician can take this opportunity to discuss the problem of convalescence with the employer and to enlist cooperation and assistance. If the clinician has had some contact with the employer during the acute phase of the patient's illness, he may have some sense of the employer's attitude toward the patient and toward psychiatric illness in general. This information may be helpful in deciding about when the patient should return to work and whether an additional call to the employer might be useful.

When the employer is reluctant to have the patient return to work, the clinician's intervention may be extremely important. Either the clinician can work towards reassuring the employer and smoothing the way for the patient to return, or it may be necessary to help the patient find other work. The clinician may need to spend time reviewing the want ads with the patient and helping to prepare him for an interview with a possible employer. For patients who have never been able to work satisfactorily, or who have disabling residual symptoms, a vocational rehabilitation program may be necessary.

Before initiating a discussion with an employer it is important to obtain the patient's consent. The patient should have a clear idea about the purpose of such a proposed conversation and is entitled to a detailed verbal report about what was said by all parties. When discussing the patient's illness with employers or teachers it is important that the clinician avoid technical terms and give reassurance sufficient to reduce apprehension about the patient's return. More familiar terms such as "depression," "emotional problems," "breakdown," and "confusion" are more likely to receive a sympathetic understanding from a layman than technical terms like "psychosis," "mania," or "schizophrenia." Patients whose jobs require that they operate machinery may need a period of careful observation before it is clear that the medication is not exposing them to the risk of injury.

Treatment During Convalescence

Treatment during the convalescent period is probably best understood as guidance, education, and active support rendered while a natural healing process takes place. The focus should be on rehabilitative and prophylactic goals. Step by step supervision of the convalescent process is necessary, particularly in the early stages. In instances where much of the early work of convalescence has been undertaken in an inpatient setting, the family may need comparatively little contact with the outpatient clinician, particularly if, at the time of outpatient referral, the patient is functioning well enough to work or to attend school. In cases where one or both parents have serious psychiatric disorders, a separate therapist may be necessary to help them to deal with their difficulties. They can still take an active role in the family treatment designed to assist the convalescing patient.

A practical, common-sense attitude is the most useful therapeutic approach in dealing with the problems of convalescence. Help with management of routine, day-to-day problems is the essence of such treatment. The patient is likely to be concerned about his capacity to function and may need encouragement and reassurance as he struggles to reestablish his confidence. Some patients set their expectations far too high, refusing to recognize any impairment and attempting tasks they were able to perform before their illness, but which are temporarily beyond their capacity. Education about the convalescent process and repeated reassurance may help to make it possible for these patients to set more realistic short-term goals.

Some patients are so convinced that they are permanently disabled that they will attempt little and take every evidence of residual symptoms, side effects, and deficits as proof that their condition is hopeless. This attitude may be associated with a withdrawn, apathetic, unmotivated state which may persist for many months. Unfortunately, there is no therapeutic maneuver which can quickly stimulate the patient to regain former levels of energy and motivated activity. More than anything else, this state seems to yield gradually to the passage of time. On the other hand, it is important that the patient lose as little ground as possible while "waiting out his convalescence." A patient who has been allowed to remain withdrawn and inactive throughout convalescence will have an especially difficult time resuming normal activity even when residual symptoms have fully receded. Individual psychotherapy is of little value in treating severely apathetic and unmotivated convalescing patients. Tedious hours filled with labored, monosyllabic comments and long silences are likely to persuade the patient and his family (quite accurately) that outpatient therapy is an expensive waste of time. In order to make any useful progress, severely apathetic patients *must* be treated with their families or in a structured setting such as a day hospital program.

Very passive and unmotivated patients do best when they are encouraged to take on a series of tasks which require a steady, reasonable degree of effort. It is the patient's continuing effort which is of importance here and even very limited goals may help keep a patient from becoming totally discouraged by providing a sense of movement and progress. The patient's family can assist in providing the encouragement and persistent gentle pressure required to prod the patient into making the necessary effort. It is important that family members and patient understand that the passivity is not under the patient's voluntary control, but that it is necessary that the patient struggle continually to overcome this inertia despite the effort it requires.

A patient who expects a period of struggle during recovery is less likely to be discouraged and uncooperative. A demoralized patient may use any combination of side effects and symptoms to justify his reluctance to make any effort to improve. Other patients may be so hampered by actual medication side effects that they think it pointless to make any effort to lead a normal existence. The therapist should acknowledge that the period is difficult and, insofar as it is possible, the dosage of medication should be adjusted to minimize problems with side effects. The patient needs help in understanding that despite these difficulties, passivity and inactivity are counterproductive and will render convalescence more difficult and prolonged.

The patient should be given credit for each small success and once a task has been successfully mastered the next assigned task should be carefully designed to be within the patient's capacities. Heroic, dramatic efforts are generally unproductive. Gentle, steady, and prudent effort at carefully graded tasks seems to provide best results. Families who are critical, demanding, and resentful of the patient are likely to make matters considerably worse. Emotional turmoil, confrontation, and intense discussions of the patient's symptoms and behavior are likely to cause a deterioration in the patient's condition. If these kinds of behavior cannot be changed in a reasonable period of time through education and family treatment, it may be necessary to help the patient make other living arrangements to reduce the risk of relapse during the convalescent period.

The tasks set for the patient with his family must be tailored to the capacities of both the family and the patient. For some patients the first goals may involve the most basic of activities, such as getting out of bed and getting dressed, attending to personal hygiene, running simple errands, or doing household chores. Other patients may need help in getting up each morning to attend school or work. For still other patients the tasks may involve participating in family activities, going on an outing, joining a club, or renewing an old friendship. Some patients are so disabled that they are unable to make use of individual treatment even at the end of convalescence. For such patients continuing family treatment or placement in a social rehabilitation program is the treatment of choice.

Once the patient is functioning reasonably well and when the family has been adequately educated and prepared, it may be possible for the clinician to begin regular individual meetings with the patient. Individual treatment must still continue to focus on day-to-day functioning. The process of educating the patient about residual symptoms, side effects, and prophylaxis against relapse must continue in the individual work. The patient can also begin the process of reviewing with the clinician the history of his illness and examining the difficulties which preceded the psychotic episode. Therapist and patient can begin to explore possible stressors in some detail, and to identify early prodromal signs of decompensation.

As the convalescent period draws to a close the patient begins to feel very much "his old self" again. Having educated the patient about his illness and in particular helped him to identify important stressors and prodromal symptoms, the patient and therapist are in a position to begin planning a longer-term strategy for protecting the patient against the risk of recurrent psychosis. In addition, the period of preparation and education can help to define areas in the patient's life that need an exploratory psychotherapeutic approach. Thus, the end of convalescence can mark a shift in the treatment from a supportive and didactic therapy to a more typical, dynamically-oriented exploratory treatment.

CHAPTER V

The Assessment of Vulnerability

EVERY RECOVERING PSYCHOTIC PATIENT runs some risk of relapse, and reducing this vulnerability is a primary task of treatment. The nonpsychotic patient enters treatment with the goal of altering some symptom or pattern of behavior which is causing distress. The recovering psychotic patient may also wish to change his life, but his treatment also has a different and often more urgent purpose—the prevention of relapse.

Ideally, therapist and patient work collaboratively using prophylactic medication and psychotherapy to minimize vulnerability to relapse, thereby making possible a stability which permits the treatment to focus on other important issues in the patient's life. In practice this collaboration is often extremely difficult to establish and maintain. The clinician should begin this process by arriving at an assessment of the patient's vulnerability to relapse. This assessment must be a clinical judgment, since there are no precise measures available to determine the risk of recurrent psychosis. The assessment must be broadly based on a careful analysis of the patient's strengths and weaknesses. Accumulating information and experience, the clinician can eventually feel a high degree of confidence in the assessment, but certainty cannot be achieved at our present level of knowledge. Consequently, this assessment must be continually adapted and revised as the clinician learns about the patient.

The patient's private assessment of his own vulnerability to relapse is a critical element that the therapist must incorporate in his assessment. Each convalescing patient constructs his own assessment of the experience of psychosis and of the risks of relapse. This self-assessment is usually fragmented and simplistic in the earliest stages of convalescence, but with continual reworking it eventually crystalizes into a more or less coherent view of the psychotic experience, its prognosis, and treatment.

As both the patient and the clinician begin to define their initial assessments of the risk of relapse, they can begin a psychotherapeutic dialogue on the subject devoted to exploring and, insofar as is possible, resolving important differences between their assessments. Clinicians often hope that this will be a simple educational process in which the therapist benevolently corrects the errors of a deferential and respectful patient. However, the reality is quite different, and the evolving dialogue on the subject may require all of the therapist's skills if it is to lead to a joint strategy for prevention of relapse.

Biologic and Psychologic Vulnerability

The clinician should begin with an initial assessment of the patient's vulnerability based on early experience with the patient and on the patient's history. In practice it may be useful for the clinician to think of vulnerability as having two dimensions: biologic and psychologic. "Biologic vulnerability" refers to the patient's endogenous or physiologic predisposition to a particular psychotic syndrome. Although this dimension cannot be assessed with precision, a careful history coupled with clinical observation can help the clinician arrive at some reasonable hypotheses. A number of factors may suggest a high level of "biologic vulnerability." For example, a strong family history of psychotic illness, early age of onset, insidious onset of psychosis, absence of clear precipitating factors, poor response to treatment, and multiple prior psychotic episodes may all suggest a high level of "biologic vulnerability."

"Psychologic vulnerability" refers to developmental, environmental, or behavioral factors which influence the risk of relapse by shaping the patient's ability to function, the likelihood of his continuing exposure to severe stressors, and the degree of his compliance with a treatment regimen. While the assessment of "biologic" factors relies primarily on information from the patient's history, the assessment of "psychologic vulnerability" is drawn primarily from exploration of the patient's views about his illness and treatment and from a growing understanding of his behavior and character as it emerges in the course of treatment.

Obviously, the distinction between "biologic" and "psychologic" vulnerability is rough and imprecise and there is considerable overlap of these two dimensions. Nonetheless, the clinician may find the distinction useful, particularly since these two dimensions often appear to vary independently. An extremely conscientious, compliant, and prudent patient may still have a high degree of "biologic" vulnerability and may relapse despite an adequate prophylactic treatment regimen. Alternatively, some severely impaired patients with little understanding of their illness and poor treatment compliance sometimes manage to live for long periods without relapse. Consequently, it is useful for the clinician to attempt to assess these dimensions separately and then combine them into a complex assessment which defines the patient's overall vulnerability.

Arrving at this overall assessment requires the weighing of a great many factors. As noted above, a careful family psychiatric history, the patient's clinical presentation during the acute phase of illness, response to medication, prior psychiatric history, and the severity of residual symptoms during convalescence may all provide important information about "biologic vulnerability."

An even broader range of factors must be considered in assessing the patient's "psychologic vulnerability." The patient's family, financial, intellectual, and educational resources are important considerations. The continuing presence and severity of important stressors, prior or current drug use, and the degree of the patient's compliance with prior psychiatric treatment are also central elements in arriving at an assessment. In addition, the severity of medication side effects and the degree of subjective distress caused by medication may be useful in estimating the patient's likely compliance with a medication regimen.

The psychiatric literature suggests that the quality of premorbid function is the best predictor of outcome following a psychotic episode. Detailed information about the patient's premorbid social skills, school or work functioning, and typical personality traits provide the clinician with information essential to developing reasonable expectations as the patient's convalescence progresses. The patient's predominant personality traits, particularly as they are reflected in understanding his illness, may play a critical role in the patient's "psychologic vulnerability." The degree to which the patient can appreciate that he has suffered a psychiatric illness, his motivation for treatment, and his conception of his vulnerability to relapse are often critical in this regard. The patient's views may determine much of his behavior in treatment, especially the ability to form a collaborative alliance with a therapist and to cooperate in a treatment regimen designed to protect him from the danger of recurrent psychosis.

Exploring the Patient's
Self-Assessment of Vulnerability

To complete the assessment of the patient's vulnerability, the clinician should begin a dialogue with the patient on the subject. Early in the convalescent period the clinician should explore the patient's conception of his vulnerability to relapse. In doing so the clinician will soon discover that most patients have learned that professionals expect them to express "correct" views about their psychotic illness. Most patients will readily repeat an "approved" version of their illness and treatment as it has been described to them. Nonetheless, many patients also are aware that the causes of psychosis are obscure and that psychotherapists often disagree about the nature and etiology of these disorders. Patients often know that diagnosis and treatment are matters of clinical judgment and that no definitive diagnostic or laboratory procedure can be done to define their illness, much less to determine with any precision their vulnerability to relapse. They usually understand that the assessment of vulnerability to relapse represents the clinician's professional opinion and that the assessment lacks the alleged authority of some types of precise medical prognostic statements.

This intrinsic imprecision does not mean that the clinician's assessment is valueless, nor that patients are as competent as clinicians in arriving at prognostic judgments. However, a clinician must keep in mind that his assessment is a hypothesis based on reasonable assumptions and that errors and misjudgments are common. Patients often object vigorously when a therapist makes dogmatic statements or describes treatment with antipsychotic medication as comparable to insulin treatment for diabetes. And the objections are valid ones. This analogy is defective in many respects, particularly because the physician who prescribes insulin can predict with a high degree of accuracy the short-term consequences of discontinuation of insulin treatment. At our current level of sophistication, we can predict with certainty neither *when* nor even *if* a postconvalescent patient will relapse if medication is stopped. We can only express a clinical judgment about the degree of risk involved in such a decision. It is worth noting that clinicians vary considerably in their estimates of vulnerability and, consequently, in their views on how long antipsychotic medication should be prescribed. Patients who consult a number of clinicians for opinions about the proper duration of treatment are likely to get widely varying responses.

Given the uncertainties involved in the assessment of vulnerability, it is not surprising that patients and families frequently feel perfectly justified in subscribing to their private assessments of the patient's illness and the need for prophylaxis against relapse. Patients may defer to a professional judgment (at least for a while), but they also remain invested in their private views. They often take pains to conceal these private assessments, fearing that the clinician will scold or lecture them for harboring foolish ideas. Only after repeated reassurance that they will not be contradicted or humiliated will patients confide their personal beliefs about the psychotic experience. On the other hand, it is often remarkable to see how pleased patients are to find that someone is genuinely interested in their opinions and willing to give them serious consideration.

Many patients spend considerable time thinking about their psychotic experience. In general, patients tend to favor a view of their disorder as transient and as the result of external and easily avoided traumata. Many can acknowledge the existence of more serious difficulties in personality or in relations with family and friends, but the significance of these difficulties is often minimized and distorted in ways that suggest that they have no bearing on the patient's possible vulnerability to relapse.

None of these conceptions should surprise the clinician. The psychotic episode is almost always a terrifying catastrophe which causes an extremely painful loss of self-esteem. Most patients only begin to become aware of the degree of their illness after they have entered convalescence. Most find the struggle to come to grips with the reality of psychosis a bewildering, depressing, and frightening ordeal. In many cases this reaction stems, in part, from the patient's realization that he was surprised by his illness and that his loss of contact with reality escaped his notice. This awareness often leads patients to frightening doubts about whether they can trust the evidence of their senses. For many patients the fear of recurrent psychosis plays a prominent, often a dominating role, in mental life during convalescence, though it is often partially or wholly unconscious.

While some patients are able to discuss their anxiety about relapse, most suppress and minimize these fears, concealing the anxiety behind a facade of confident self-assurance.

The Dimensions of Insight*

A patient's conceptions of the psychotic experience are complex phenomena usually described by the term "insight." There are in fact a number of distinct dimensions of insight, each relatively independent of the others and with differing impact on the patient's behavior in treatment. The acknowledgment of having suffered a psychiatric illness is most basic, and patients vary greatly in their capacity to achieve this awareness. A minority of patients steadfastly deny any illness whatsoever, and they may insist that their problems were the result of malice or misunderstanding. However, most patients admit some degree of illness, although they often minimize its severity. Some patients with high levels of denial may refuse treatment altogether, although many are willing to enter treatment despite their denial.

Many patients who deny that they have suffered a mental illness are able to describe their psychotic symptoms freely and in detail, although they insist that the symptoms do not represent an illness. In these cases the denial of illness may permit the patient to minimize his fear of psychosis and reduce his sense of being stigmatized by the label of mental illness. These patients may therefore be compliant patients and remain on antipsychotic medication for a period of time without acknowledging that doing so represents a contradiction of their denial. The clinician should of course take care not to confront such a patient directly with this contradiction, since to do so might force him to terminate treatment. Gradual exploration of the

*The content of this section is largely drawn from an ongoing clinical research project in which Malcolm Bowers, John Strauss, and Marshal Mandelkern are coinvestigators with the author.

patient's concerns about relapse and stigma may make it possible for the patient to accept the fact of psychotic illness and to participate more fully in the treatment.

The capacity to acknowledge and describe psychotic symptoms is a separate dimension of insight. Some patients can describe symptoms in detail but deny that they have suffered a mental illness. Conversely, some patients can acknowledge that they have suffered a major psychiatric illness but still distort, deny, or minimize some or all of the psychotic symptoms they experienced. These patients describe a serious psychriatric disorder which differs greatly from the clinician's observations, yet such patients may be quite willing to enter into treatment for assistance with their problems as they have come to define them. They may be very much concerned about relapse and will often comply with a proposed medication regimen. However, their inability to identify and discuss psychotic symptoms may make it difficult for them to define appropriate target symptoms to monitor. The therapist may find it impossible to educate them properly about the purposes of antipsychotic medication and they may be unable to identify prodromal signs of impending decompensation. As a result, these patients may be unable to assume any responsibility for the management of their medication later in treatment. Fortunately, exploratory psychotherapeutic effort can often make it possible for these patients to reach a more realistic view of the nature of their illness and its symptoms.

Patients who deny or greatly minimize both their symptoms and the fact that they suffered a mental illness are frequently inaccessible to treatment, or nearly so. It is a taxing technical challenge for a clinician to treat a patient who, for the most part, insists he has no illness or symptoms requiring treatment. Any of the therapist's attempts to persuade such a patient to the contrary will be met by stiff resistance. In such a situation the clinician can only try to engage the patient on comparatively neutral topics in the hope that he or she will eventually feel more secure. The therapeutic alliance in such cases is tenuous at best. If the patient will tolerate a discussion of antipsychotic medication, its use is best presented as a conservative precaution designed to prevent possible future difficulty.

A 23-year-old student was admitted to a short-term psychiatric hospital ward after barricading herself in her dormitory room. At the time of her admission she was suffering from auditory hallucinations, persecutory delusions, and marked looseness of associations. She was treated with antipsychotic medication and was discharged from the hospital after one month.

She arranged to take a semester off from school and to work while beginning her outpatient treatment. Shortly after discharge her clinician asked her to describe the events and symptoms which led to her hospitalization. It was clear that she had markedly distorted her recollections. She described becoming increasingly depressed and told of becoming gradually withdrawn from classmates and school activities. She admitted to difficulties with sleep and concentration, but denied all other symptoms. When reminded, for example, about her problem with "hearing voices," she could recall only that she had been preoccupied with self-critical thoughts. She was unable to recall her hallucinations or delusions, nor did she recall the degree of disorganization and confusion she had suffered at the time of her admission to the hospital. For example, she could recall only that she had wanted desperately to be left alone, but was unable to remember that she had barricaded herself in her room.

She explained that she regarded her difficulties as an intense, but understandable, reaction to the stresses of her school work and that she did not consider herself to have suffered a mental illness. She did acknowledge that she might need some brief counseling to help her deal with her relations with peers and with her school problems and she agreed to enter outpatient psychotherapy for this purpose. However, she discontinued both her medication and her treatment after a few months. Several months later she suffered a recurrence of similar psychotic symptoms, resulting in a second hospitalization.

This patient distorted and minimized the whole of her recollection of the psychotic experience and she saw little reason for treatment to protect her against recurrent psychosis. Because she was unable to acknowledge her illness or symptoms in any useful way, her clinician might reasonably conclude that her psychological vulnerability to relapse was high.

A patient's conception of the causes of his disorder is another important dimension of insight. Even patients who deny
illness and symptoms altogether must still have some explanation for their presence in a hospital or a psychotherapist's office. The most terrified and resistant patients frequently are
those who seem most convinced that they have fully understood the causes of their disorder. Less defensive patients are,
typically, genuinely puzzled about the causes of their illness
and often have more complex and tentative hypotheses about
it. Patients may invoke heredity, physical illness, drugs, toxic
hypothesis, family difficulties, school or work problems, sexual
difficulties, loneliness, and many other problems as likely
causes of their disorder. Since patients typically prefer a view
of their illness which characterizes it as transient and limited,
they tend to favor causal hypotheses which support this view.
Thus toxic hypotheses ("someone must have slipped me some
LSD," "I must have had a very high fever,") or simple stress
hypotheses ("I didn't get enough sleep—I was exhausted," "I
pushed myself too hard and got overextended") predominate.

Many patients can also acknowledge more substantial problems or stressors that contributed to the onset of their psychotic
illness. Patients may describe school or work difficulties, family
problems, or difficulties in their relationships with friends and
lovers which caused them great pain and which contributed to
their decompensation. Where there is a strong family history of
serious psychiatric illness, patients may feel that heredity has
played a central role in the development of illness and they
may feel "doomed" to a life of chronic psychiatric disability.
Many patients are aware that drug use contributed in important ways to their decompensation. These patients also may be
aware that loneliness, difficulties in personal relationships, or
other problems were important pressures which led them to
seek relief in drug use.

The patient's conception of the nature and efficacy of treatment is another important dimension of insight. For example,
many patients are aware that medication helps to control their
symptoms. Such patients may have great faith in medication as

an effective prophylactic agent against recurrent psychosis. However, many other patients have a confused or limited sense of the role of medication, while some may only be aware of the undesirable side effects of medication and may detect no beneficial effect whatever. Patients may also have strong views about the need for psychotherapeutic treatment. Many patients understand that they need assistance, but other patients may feel strongly that they prefer to struggle with their problems alone and that the clinician is an intruder who must be warded off.

The last dimension of insight is the patient's assessment of his vulnerability to recurrent psychosis. Each patient draws some conclusions about vulnerability and about his capacity to control and minimize that vulnerability. Even during the early stages of convalescence most patients form some sense of how much they are at risk. Most patients cannot tolerate the idea that relapse may be a likely possibility. They generally struggle to remain optimistic and most are able to do so. Exceptions are patients who have had multiple psychotic episodes and have grown hopeless about preventing them, as well as those with strong family histories of psychosis. Some patients insist that the risk is negligible and that they need take no precautions. This is especially true of grandiose patients. In particular, patients with bipolar disorders tend to see themselves as invulnerable to relapse. However, most patients are aware that some prophylaxis is necessary and are willing to discuss the matter in a continuing way in treatment. Usually, however, they minimize the risk and press for only short-term prophylactic treatment.

Each of these aspects of the patient's insight regarding his illness and its treatment is useful to the clinician in arriving at an overall, clinical estimate of the patient's psychologic vulnerability to relapse. The patient's opinions about each of these areas helps to define major disagreements between the clinician and patient and to suggest difficulties which might arise if the patient develops prodromal symptoms of psychosis. It seems likely that the patient's views about his illness permit clinicians, in a limited way, to predict the likely degree of the patient's compliance with a proposed treatment regimen.

Patterns of Insight

The examples which follow offer the reader a small sample of the variety and richness patients present to clinicians attempting to assess vulnerability. In each instance a constellation of factors provides the clinician with a rough estimate of vulnerability, which in turn is useful in helping the clinician to formulate an initial treatment strategy.

Jennie is a 21-year-old single college student with no prior psychiatric history. She was admitted to a short-term psychiatric ward from a hospital emergency room with a chief complaint of ''I think I was psychotic.'' For several months prior to her admission she reported a series of ''strange experiences.'' These included ''religious experiences, increased anxiety, a conviction that other students were conspiring against her, visual distortions, auditory hallucinations, and grandiose delusions.'' During the week prior to admission the symptoms gradually worsened and eventually she became agitated and disorganized.

A number of stressful events preceded this decompensation. A maternal aunt, a strong and central figure in her family, had died four months previously. As a college senior she was struggling with decisions about her career choices following graduation. She was considering applying to graduate programs but was unable to decide which course of study she preferred. She was very much involved with her boyfriend, also a college senior. He, too, was struggling with anxiety about graduation and it was not clear that their relationship would continue. The patient also reported feeling pressured and overextended at school.

The patient's older sister had suffered two psychotic episodes. This sister had slowly deteriorated, particularly after the second episode and her compliance with treatment had been poor. An older brother and the patient's father also have a history of ''emotional problems'' although they never had formal psychiatric treatment. Jennie grew up in an ambitious and successful middle-class family. She did well at school and her parents had high expectations for her. Although she lived in the college dormitory, her school was within commuting distance of her parents' home. On several occasions she had spent holidays away from her family, but she had never been out of commuting distance for any substantial period of time.

Jennie was treated with antipsychotic medication and lithium. She had a good response to treatment and over a period of several weeks in the hospital most of her symptoms receded. After discharge to outpatient care she was able to acknowledge fully her psychotic symptoms and to identify them as part of a definite psychotic illness. In fact, she appeared to be aware of her illness from the onset. She was of the opinion that the combination of her aunt's death, her concerns about her relationship with her boyfriend, and overwork at school had combined to precipitate her illness. However, she had no sense that her impending graduation, her difficulty with career choices, and the prospect of separation from her family played any role in her illness.

She was aware that medication had led to a rapid remission of her symptoms and she felt that psychotherapy would be useful to monitor her condition and to help her avoid difficulty. She expressed a marked fear of relapse, but felt that her awareness and her continuing treatment would provide adequate protection.

Jennie is a remarkable patient in that she demonstrated an unusually high level of insight into her illness both in the acute and convalescent phases of treatment. She is not unusual in her ability to describe her symptoms accurately, but her capacity to recognize these as symptoms of psychotic illness from the time of her admission is unusual and perhaps related to having observed her sister's illness. She is aware of the risk of relapse and relies on medication and treatment to protect her. As a result, she is likely to be a reliable and compliant patient. Although her speculations about the causes of her illness avoid some emotionally charged issues, the prospects for enlarging her understanding of these factors through exploratory psychotherapy seems good. Given the likelihood of her compliance with a treatment regimen and her interest in exploring problem areas, it seems that her psychologic vulnerability to relapse is low.

However, her family history suggests a possible high level of biologic vulnerability to illness despite her high levels of insight and excellent engagement in treatment. A number of members of her immediate family have had "emotional difficulties" and her sister has had two psychotic episodes similar to Jennie's. This sort of family history might suggest that Jennie's prophylactic antipsychotic medication should be continued for a longer than usual period of time. In fact, premature discontinuation of medication proved to be a serious problem in her treatment.

> Since she had residual cognitive difficulties during convalescence, Jennie took a semester off from school at the recommendation of her clinician. She took a clerical job and returned to her parents' home. When she returned to school the following semester she did extremely well, approaching her premorbid level of function. Several months after she returned to school her clinician suggested that she could safely discontinue medications. Jennie expressed some concerns about stopping medication, pointing out that graduation was approaching and that she was likely to find it stressful. The clinician reassured her, insisting that she was doing well enough to manage without prophylactic medication and that her understanding of her illness would make it possible for her to recognize early signs of any difficulty which might arise. Three weeks after discontinuing her medication she developed (over a three day period) a full-blown recurrence of psychotic symptoms requiring one month of hospital treatment.

Despite her high level of insight, excellent treatment compliance, and excellent functioning at school the discontinuation of medications was clearly an error. Her high level of biologic vulnerability made continued prophylaxis with medication an essential part of her treatment. This being the case, a more conservative treatment strategy with prolonged medication prophylaxis would have been indicated. Given her high level of insight and treatment compliance, she could probably be expected to understand the discussion of the risks of relapse and to agree to conservative management. Considering the fact that she was approaching graduation from college with the major decisions and changes that entailed, continuation of prophylactic medication through the transition would obviously have been more prudent. Even if Jennie had no history of serious family psychopathology, discontinuing medication shortly before major life changes was an unreasonably risky plan.

Mary, a 25-year-old, was referred for outpatient treatment after three months of hospitalization for an acute psychotic illness characterized by profound disorganization, loose associations, agitation, delusions, and hallucinations. She had been hospitalized for similar symptoms on two previous occasions, with the second hospitalization lasting nearly one year. Her adjustment between hospitalizations was marginal and medication compliance was poor. During the three months of her most recent hospitalization she was treated with antipsychotic medication and intensive milieu therapy. Her response was gradual and incomplete. At the time of her discharge from the hospital she was still mildly disorganized and painfully depressed. With some assistance she was able to find a roommate to share an apartment and found work as a waitress. She remained depressed, apathetic, and extremely pessimistic about her future.

Her father is a successful attorney, her mother a withdrawn and eccentric woman who seldom leaves her house. An older brother was hospitalized after a suicide attempt. Over the years her parents had come to see Mary as too ill to profit from treatment and they had begun to share her pessimism about her future.

Mary was able to describe her symptoms in great detail and regarded herself as doomed to a life of chronic psychotic illness. She viewed herself as defective and therefore powerless to alter the course of her illness. Cynical about her previous treatment, she had come to view psychotherapy as pathetically ineffective and medication as a palliative agent of extremely limited value. Three episodes of prolonged psychosis had made this young woman painfully aware of the severity of her illness. While she was able to describe her psychotic episodes in great detail, she found these recollections exquisitely embarrassing and stigmatizing. She was convinced that her illness was caused by her inability to tolerate the ordinary stresses of life. She minimized family and interpersonal problems, emphasizing instead her sense of inadequacy and fragility.

This patient is all too aware of the severity of her illness and her vulnerability to recurrent psychosis. Her pessimism about her future led to a profound demoralization which was the major initial focus of her treatment. Although demoralization occurs most frequently in patients who have suffered repeated psychotic episodes, it can occur in patients who are recovering from their first psychotic break as well. It is usually accompanied by a profound constriction of personality and affect. Depression is also a prominent part of demoralization and in severe cases may be of suicidal proportions. In any case, passivity, withdrawal, and apathy are characteristic of these patients and these factors may be the major reasons for poor treatment compliance.

The fear of recurrent psychosis loomed so large in Mary's mind that she took great pains to avoid any emotional arousal. She was intensely frightened of any strange sensation or experience. She was inclined to exaggerate her vulnerability to relapse and to seek repeated reassurance for minor symptoms of anxiety or excitement. Her convalescence took several years and considerable reassurance, support, and encouragement were necessary before her pessimism and anxiety about relapse began to abate. It was only after several years had elapsed that she began to be less preoccupied with fears of recurrent psychosis. She was conscientiously compliant with her treatment regimen. In fact, she was needy and dependent on treatment and reluctant to reduce the dosage of her medication. Similarly, she had great difficulty tolerating her therapist's vacations. Surges of anxiety about relapse occasionally prompted her to seek extra sessions or increases in medication.

After four years of treatment she began active, exploratory work in psychotherapy and began to approach changes in her life with some tentative energy and enthusiasm. Early in her treatment she agreed with her therapist that indefinite treatment with prophylactic antipsychotic medication was likely to be necessary. However, the dose was gradually reduced to a modest maintenance level. In the fifth year of her treatment she was able to discontinue the medication with the understanding that it would be resumed if any change in her clinical state suggested that she was in danger of relapse.

Mary's anxiety and pessimism about relapse made her a cooperative and compliant patient. Her emotional constriction and anxiety initially had some value in protecting her against behavior which might put her at risk for relapse. However, the constriction and demoralization eventually became themselves major stressors in that they prevented movement and progress in her treatment. Fortunately, she was able to overcome some of her pessimism and begin a more active exploratory treatment. Although her multiple psychotic episodes suggest high levels of biologic vulnerability, her painful awareness of her vulnerability to relapse made her a conscientious patient whose psychologic vulnerability was consequently comparatively low.

In some other patients the situation is markedly different, with apparently low levels of biologic vulnerability but high psychologic vulnerability to recurrent psychosis. These patients present a different set of technical problems for the clinician involved in their treatment.

Sarah is a 40-year-old divorced woman, living with her two teenage children in a rural town. She is unemployed and receives state aid and alimony for her support. She has a 10th grade education and a sporadic work history. At 27 she suffered an acute psychotic episode with pronounced somatic delusions, social withdrawal, and depressive symptoms, culminating in a suicide attempt which led to a two month stay in a state hospital.

Several years after that episode she was in treatment briefly in an outpatient clinic setting. She apparently sought treatment at the instigation of her husband when he sensed that she was in difficulty. On that occasion she was willing to take antipsychotic medication for a limited period of time. Her last contact with a mental health professional was eight years before her second psychotic episode.

At the age of 39 Sarah separated from her husband of 20 years. Divorce was granted six months later with Sarah receiving custody of her children. Ten days prior to her second admission to a psychiatric hospital her children noted that her behavior was becoming more and more bizarre. She played loud music in the early morning hours, mumbled incoherently, and carried on conversations with imaginary figures. On the day of admission she went to her neighbor's home and with considerable agitation declared that aliens were invading the earth. She was taken to an emergency room and hospitalized on a 15-day certificate. In the hospital she was treated with antipsychotic medication and within a few days was considerably better. At that time she signed into the hospital voluntarily.

Antipsychotic medication led to a gradual, but reasonably complete suppression of her psychotic symptoms. After one month she was discharged for follow-up in the hospital's outpatient clinic. At the time of her discharge she was able to discuss many of the events that led to her psychotic episode but she distorted and minimized the most severe of her symptoms. "I had a slight breakdown. It wasn't so bad as the one 13 years ago. I did a lot of singing and I got pretty mixed up because I was so happy. My ex-husband came to visit me and that surprised me. We drank some whiskey together and since I don't drink, the bottle was a very old one that may have been standing around the cupboard for years. I think maybe the whiskey had gone bad, because it sent me on a terrible bad trip. The bad trip got very scary and I got pretty panicky and mixed up. I had a lot of strange ideas. Sometimes I think all of them might still be true, but other times it all seems like a dream. I don't think I'm really seriously sick. The whiskey is what did it to me. I don't have any serious problems in my life. I guess I was a little upset about the divorce, but I don't think it really caused my breakdown."

"I feel I have completely recovered now. It helps me to have someone to talk to and I suppose I'll need treatment for a little while. The medicine helped me relax a bit and it helps me to sleep, but sometimes I think it just makes me fat and dull. I don't think treatment is really necessary. I might be wrong but I don't think I need medicine at all. I'm inclined to try going without it for a while to see what happens. You never know for sure about these things, but I don't think I'm in danger of a relapse and anyway there's no way to prevent one if it's coming. What I really need is to find a man to live with. That would help me more than anything."

Sarah has had two widely separated psychotic episodes. It also seems possible that at least one additional psychotic episode was prevented by timely outpatient treatment most likely instigated by her husband. Even her short-term compliance with treatment was relatively poor. This history suggests a comparatively low level of biologic vulnerability. On the other hand, her psychologic vulnerability to relapse seems high. In addition to her limited understanding of her illness and poor history of treatment compliance, her work history is not encouraging and she has limited financial and social resources. There are now no mature stable family members she can call upon for support or assistance in monitoring her psychological state. Although she can describe her illness with a degree of accuracy, her denial is quite strong. Her conviction that "bad whiskey" leading to a "bad trip" was responsible for her psychotic episode makes it likely that she will continue to be poor in her compliance with any proposed treatment.

Apparently the isolation and loneliness resulting from Sarah's recent separation and divorce were the major life changes that precipitated her current psychotic episode. This stress is likely to continue for some time, making her considerably more vulnerable in the immediate future. Although she accepted a referral for outpatient treatment, Sarah made it clear from the outset that she expected her treatment to be brief, perhaps no more than a few visits. She also made it clear that she was especially concerned about her attractiveness and her tendency to gain weight on antipsychotic medication. Since she regards the problem of finding a male companion as her first priority, she views a prolonged course of prophylactic antipsychotic medication as counter to her best interests.

Given this constellation of factors the clinician can focus attention on attempts to engage Sarah in treatment in ways that she finds acceptable. For example, the therapist might set the goal of negotiating an agreement with her so she would continue on a reduced level of antipsychotic medication for a limited period of time. After that the therapist might propose that she discontinue medication and that they meet regularly for monitoring of her clinical state. Her teenage children are struggling to disengage themselves from a sense of responsibility and guilt with regard to their mother's illness and it would not be fair or proper to ask them to assist in monitoring her condition or to take any responsibility for participating in her treatment. In fact, the children may need assistance in dealing with their guilt about separating themselves from their mother and in establishing lives and careers for themselves outside their mother's home. Although the clinician might feel that Sarah's vulnerability is increased by the early discontinuation of anti-psychotic medication, that compromise might be well worthwhile if it permitted the patient to continue in treatment. Psychotherapy might initially focus on her difficulties in finding a male companion, a subject of great importance to her and which she might be interested in pursuing actively in treatment. This might permit her to become gradually engaged in treatment, thereby making it possible for her to be monitored on a regular basis.

> Steve, a 22-year-old single man, was hospitalized for the treatment of an acute psychotic disorder characterized by grandiose delusions, auditory hallucinations, and formal thought disorder. After graduating from high school he had enlisted in the armed forces and was honorably discharged one year prior to his decompensation. After his discharge he enrolled as a student in a technical school in a neighboring state. He managed to pass each of his courses at school but found them stressful and difficult. Approximately three months prior to his hospital admission he took a leave of absence from school to "begin working on several private projects." Although he continued living in the same town where his school was located, he gradually withdrew from social contacts with his former classmates and spent his time alone in his room.
>
> One month prior to his hospital admission he abruptly returned to his parents' home. They were shocked to find him massively disorganized and delusional. At their insistence he reluctantly began outpatient treatment and a trial of antipsychotic medication. His symptoms failed to respond to this regimen and three weeks later he was admitted to the hospital. At the time of his admission he was preoccupied with messianic delusions, believing that he had invented a variety of marvels which would transform human society. He was withdrawn, nearly mute, guarded, and suspicious.
>
> Steven had no family history of psychiatric illness and no prior history of mental illness or treatment. He was described by his parents as a shy, gentle person who did average work in

school and who was usually found on the periphery of social life. He responded very gradually to large doses of antipsychotic medication. After two months in the hospital he was functioning reasonably well and was able to return to his parents' home to begin looking for a job. At the time he was referred for outpatient treatment he was able to acknowledge that he had suffered a mental illness. However, he minimized and distorted his recollections of his symptoms. He did remember mistakenly believing that he had invented some amazing machines. "I still firmly believe that I am quite capable of inventing these things, though I know now that I haven't already done so. I think my breakdown was caused by overwork and too much pressure at school. I wasn't eating right. Too much junk food upsets your body chemistry. I don't have any other problems. I know I can do well because I am convinced I have great talent as an inventor."

While he admitted that there was an extremely remote possibility of relapse, he felt certain that only modest preventive measures were in order. A few months of medication and psychotherapy would suffice, he believed, to protect him from any possibility of relapse in the foreseeable future.

Although he was aware that he suffered a serious psychiatric illness, Steven otherwise had comparatively little insight into his condition. He minimized his symptoms and harbored some grandiose beliefs about his potential. He had little sense about the stresses which precipitated his illness and had not yet come to grips with the fact that he found school too difficult and was now forced to struggle with painful questions about his future. His social skills were limited and he had no supporting network of friends to tide him over this difficult time. His poor insight and lack of engagement in treatment suggest high psychologic vulnerability to relapse.

On the other hand, the presence of intact, responsible, and supportive parents makes his treatment prospects brighter. Since he planned to live with his parents during convalescence, they must play a major role in his treatment. The therapist's alliance with them is likely to be crucial to maintaining Steven in treatment. A prolonged period of family treatment may be necessary in order to keep this patient on prophylactic medication and involved in the treatment process. Eventually it may be possible for Steven to develop a strong enough working alliance with his therapist to make it feasible for the two of them to begin working alone. The initial family work may make it possible for Steven to begin working at a regular job appropriate to his skills and limitations. Once he is steadily employed his treatment can begin to address his disappointment with his prospects and his limited career choices. At this point individual treatment may be especially useful. Eventually, his individual treatment can begin to address his longstanding concerns with loneliness and social isolation.

Unfortunately, high levels of insight into a psychotic illness do not necessarily protect a patient from relapse unless considerable psychotherapeutic effort has been focused on the problem of early identification of prodromal symptoms. In addition, many patients, particularly those with bipolar disorders, tend to lose even high levels of insight fairly rapidly once they enter a prodromal phase of psychosis. This rapid loss of insight may lead patients to avoid medication and treatment at precisely the moment when it is most necessary.

Henry, a 21-year-old single college sophomore, suffered his second manic episode while studying for his final examinations at school. His first psychotic episode occurred just before the spring holiday during his freshman year. He had done well at school up until that point, although he was somewhat isolated socially and had difficulty finding girls to date. His stay at school was also the first time that he was away from his parents for any substantial period of time. About six weeks prior to the first episode he experienced increased anxiety and social withdrawal, and decreased appetite. He gradually began to sense a change in himself and in the appearance of the world around him. He had difficulty concentrating on his work and stayed up very late to complete his school assignments. During the week prior to his hospitalization he experienced ideas of reference which gradually increased in severity until they became frank psychotic delusions.

At the time of his admission he was preoccupied with grandiose delusions and was suffering auditory and visual hallucinations. At that time he was incoherent, elated, and hypersexual. It was only after two weeks of treatment with antipsychotic medication and lithium that he began to calm down and to acknowledge that he was ill and in a psychiatric hospital. At one point during the first days of his hospitalization his agitation required that he be placed in restraints, and hospital security guards were summoned to assist the ward nursing staff. During this process one of the security guards told him, ''I'm so sorry that you're having all these problems.'' Henry's outraged response was ''What problems?!''

Over the succeeding weeks Henry improved greatly. He was able to gradually accept the fact that he had been ill and that he would need continued inpatient treatment. As his condition improved he became interested in learning more about his illness and he used his considerable intelligence to educate himself about every aspect of bipolar disorders and their treatment. He placed great faith in his medication and entered enthusiastically into outpatient treatment.

He took a semester off from school and worked at a local bookstore. After six months of outpatient treatment he felt ready to return to college. His therapist agreed that he was doing extremely well and his neuroleptic medication was discontinued approximately six weeks before he left to resume his college education. He arranged to continue on lithium and to be followed every week by a college counselor who would monitor his clinical condition and his medication.

Approximately three weeks prior to the second admission he began experiencing a change in his mood and he became preoccupied with worries about sexual matters. He slept somewhat less, was more withdrawn socially, and had some difficulty concentrating on his school work. He noticed that the world was beginning to look somehow strange and different to him. However, by the time he recognized that these changes had occurred, he was also elated and ''felt better than ever.'' ''I realized that all of my earlier thoughts about my special powers had been correct and that I mistakenly thought I was an ordinary person. I realized that the medication made me doubt myself and that I was in fact the unique and extraordinary person I always hoped I was.'' He skipped his appointment with his therapist and took lithium only intermittently over the next several weeks. At the time of his second hospital admission he was again grossly delusional, pressured, elated, and hypersexual.

In this instance, Henry's high level of insight into his disorder was of little use in helping him to avoid a recurrence of his psychotic illness. The fact that he had so little insight during his initial episode provides the only hint that this "loss of insight" might well be a problem again during a second episode.

Bipolar patients with this problem may need considerable help in understanding that their insight is fragile and may be lost quickly during a hypomanic prodromal phase of psychosis when quick action is required. A patient, who is forewarned that he will likely disagree with the recommendation to resume or increase medication, may be able to accept that recommendation despite a loss of insight at the critical moment. In any case, such patients may need a prolonged period of psychotherapeutic work spanning several such prodromal periods or even several relapses into psychotic illness before they can learn to monitor adequately their own clinical state.

Henry did well during his second hospitalization and he was discharged on lithium and a moderate dose of neuroleptic medication. Once again he worked for a semester before returning to school. This time he continued to take both lithium and a low maintenance dose of neuroleptic medication throughout the year after his second decompensation. However, during the following year he became increasingly confident about his stability and concerned about the risk of tardive dyskinesia. He began to press his clinician to discontnue the neuroleptic. Since his second psychotic episode occurred following discontinuation of neuroleptic medication, his clinician was understandably hesitant to risk a third decompensation and he advised his patient to continue on both medications. However, Henry was so insistent that the clinician ultimately felt obliged to negotiate a compromise in which both parties agreed to discontinue the neuroleptic over a six month period while continuing treatment with lithium.

About two months after the neuroleptic medication was discontinued altogether Henry developed prodromal symptoms for the third time. He slept little and became preoccupied, irritable, and overactive. This time he was able to recognize the fact that he was in difficulty before frank psychotic symptoms occurred. He called his therapist and suggested that "I might need a rest in the hospital. The world is looking different to me and I realize I've been doing some inappropriate things." After an emergency session with his clinician later that day, Henry signed himself into the hospital. However, immediately after admission he pronounced himself ''perfectly well'' and he refused all medication. It was only after several hours of persuasion that he relented and agreed to take the prescribed medication. He made rapid progress and was able to leave the hospital after a comparatively short stay. Following this experience he was able to understand the need for continued treatment with low dose neuroleptic medication.

Henry's growing capacity to be aware of prodromal symptoms may make it possible for him to try again later to discontinue neuroleptic medication. Since many patients like Henry are able to remain stable on lithium alone once they reach their late twenties, he may be able to discontinue the neuroleptic after several stable years on both agents. In addition, Henry's growing ability to recognize prodromal symptoms may make it possible for him to monitor his clinical state and regulate intermittent use of neuroleptics on his own. However, many such patients need to be monitored carefully by others on an indefinite basis because, despite their best efforts, the earliest manifestations of their illness distort their judgment in ways which make self-regulation of medication impossible.

CHAPTER VI

The Meanings of Medication

PRESCRIBING MEDICATION for a patient is an act charged with meaning and rich in associations. For most physicians the daily routine of clinical practice obscures awareness of the fantasies and intense feelings created by the transaction. It often appears that both patients and physicians have come to take medical science for granted and overlook the powerful expectations evoked when medication is prescribed.

Attitudes Toward Medicines

Psychotic Patients and the Traditional Medical Model

Patients with physical illnesses usually share with their physicians a common conception of illness and of scientific medical treatment. This shared conception is usually the basis for the patient's trust in his physician and for his willingness to become a collaborator in treatment. As in psychotherapy, successful treatment of physical illness ultimately depends on an active therapeutic alliance between clinician and patient, at least to the extent of compliance with a proposed medication regimen. However, despite the similarity between medical and psychotherapeutic models of treatment, there are in practice some important differences between them regarding the prescription of medication; differences stemming primarily from some unique aspects of psychiatric illness and its treatment.

Patients who seek medical treatment for physical illness usually expect that medication will be prescribed, consider themselves ill and are prepared to accept the physician's assessment that treatment is required. There is a shared system of beliefs between patient and physician about the nature of illness and about indications for treatment. Although doubts and reservations may exist, patients are usually willing to regard the physician as an expert who can diagnose illness and prescribe proper and specific treatment. Such patients can assume with confidence that most other physicians would arrive at the same diagnosis and propose similar or identical treatment (even if they need to believe their physician is somehow ''the best'').

Psychotic patients are often aware that matters are considerably different with regard to the treatment of psychotic illness. They know that psychotherapists often differ widely on matters of diagnosis and treatment and that indications for the use of medication are based on clinical judgments rather than on definitive diagnostic procedures. As a result, the prescription of medication for such patients usually requires considerable explanation and discussion. Other factors contribute to differences in patients' attitudes towards antipsychotic medications compared with prescriptions for physical illnesses. Whatever fears he may have about illness and treatment, the patient with a physical disorder is secure in the knowledge that large areas of his personal and psychic life will play no direct part in the treatment. However, psychotic patients are likely to imagine that every aspect of their personal life, family relationships, values, sexual habits and preferences, private fantasy life, and their psychic integrity are (or should be) at stake in the treatment. Such patients are likely to approach the therapist with a good deal of caution and suspicion about the use of any proposed psychotropic medication.

Psychotic patients also differ from patients suffering from other psychiatric disorders. Patients suffering from neurotic symptoms or depressive disorders are usually aware of their symptoms and can acknowledge that their distress may be of psychological origin. They often have a degree of awareness of the pressures and conflicts which might have contributed to their distress, and they may agree that these difficulties require treatment. In any case, they are generally able to conceive of a prescribed medication as possibly useful in relieving symptoms and may even request medication to help relieve those symptoms. For the most part they view medication as designed for the temporary relief of symptoms and they do not expect it to produce any fundamental change in their personality.

Psychotic patients may have a much more limited conception of their disorder. Antipsychotic medication also differs fundamentally from other psychotropic medications designed to relieve symptoms of anxiety or depression. Antipsychotic medication directly alters the organization and content of the patient's thoughts and perceptions. When used in the treatment of psychosis these agents often have a profound effect on a patient's sense of self. From this perspective, antipsychotic medication represents the most intimate of possible intrusions on the part of the clinician into the very center of the patient's consciousness. Most patients are properly wary of such an intrusion. A confused and suspicious psychotic patient is especially likely to be frightened about the implications and consequences of treatment with these agents. The difficulty is compounded by the psychotic patient's frequent uncertainty about his illness. Explanations about the purposes of medication are not very convincing if the patient doesn't feel convinced that his problems are psychological in origin. Given the perception that so much is at stake in the decisions about medication and the confusions about whether medication is necessary, it is not surprising that disorganized and suspicious psychotic patients resist taking antipsychotic medication and that discussions about medicine between patient and therapist are frequently difficult, and prolonged.

Covert Meanings of Medication

Much of the initial resistance to antipsychotic medication is caused by fears resulting from misinformation. Both patient and family require a persistent educational effort by the therapist to provide them with a factual understanding of the purposes and risks involved in the use of these medicines. However, clinicians soon learn that even apparently intelligent and knowledgeable patients and families often stubbornly resist these educational efforts. This remarkable and exasperating phenomenon is sometimes immediately apparent in the interchange between patient, family, and clinician, while at other times it remains covert. Patient and family may appear to accept the clinician's views and recommendations, only to gradually (and often secretly) reduce dosages or discontinue use of medication altogether.

In these cases the difficulty is not a failure of educational method, and the lack of compliance cannot be remedied by more vigorous or persuasive didactic effort. This is because medication frequently is invested with a wide variety of other (frequently unconscious) meanings and associations, which are personal and, of course, vary greatly from patient to patient, and from family to family. Despite this variability there are some common concerns and themes which therapists are likely to encounter with some frequency. In many cases the successful exploration of these unconscious meanings of or fantasies about medication may be a critical element in overcoming a patient's resistance to taking medication as part of treatment.

Like any psychotherapeutic issue, this exploration should be approached with tact, respect, and a thoughtful sensitivity to appropriate pace. Unlike other explorations, investigation of resistance to the use of medication cannot be neutral, since the patient already knows that the therapist has recommended the medication. Inevitably, patients perceive psychotherapeutic work on this issue as the therapist's attempt to persuade the patient to take the medication. Under such circumstances, useful exploratory work can be done only if patients are genuinely convinced that they are free to make a choice about the use of medication. The clinician should remember that the patient has the right to refuse medication, as indeed the patient has a right to refuse any aspect of treatment. Thus, the clinician's approach to the discussions about resistance to medication should convey clearly that the patient has a choice in the matter, even though the therapist has recommended its use.

In these discussions, the therapist's restraint and patience can often bear rich rewards. A patient who feels he has genuinely chosen a clinical trial of medication is usually willing to discuss his reactions to the medication, his degree of the adherence to the dosage schedule, and his fears and fantasies about the medication throughout the duration of treatment. The clinician should avoid the temptation to override the patient's hesitancy, simply directing him to take the medicine. A directed patient may agree to comply with the prescribed treatment, but is likely to harbor a lingering sense of not having been consulted adequately. In addition, such patients regard therapy as something done to them, rather than with them. Inevitably, this provokes resentment and alienation in the patient. The therapeutic alliance suffers and each dose of medication may rekindle the resentment and conflict. The result is some disruption of the treatment, which may range from a covert or overt failure of compliance with some aspect of the treatment regimen to continuing complaints about the medication, the psychotherapy, or the therapist.

"Moral Objections"

A common type of resistance to antipsychotic medication can be best described by the term ''moral objection.'' Patients and family members may harbor the idea that psychiatric illness is a form of "weakness" and that the taking of medication in its treatment compounds that weakness. Patients of this sort are humiliated by their condition and any proposed medication entails additional humiliation and self-contempt. These patients are likely to regard use of medication as a kind of "crutch" or "a giving in to the illness."

Therapists are often puzzled by this moralistic tendency on the part of patients and their family members. Clinicians may even feel offended by the implication that somehow they are trying to "corrupt" their patients by "tempting them to take the easy way out" via a mind altering drug. The therapist should bear in mind that although the use of medication for pain is common, much emphasis is placed in our culture on the "immorality" of *relying* on drugs for the relief of psychological distress. For example, young people hear repeatedly about the "cowardice" and "escapism" of people who use alcohol or drugs to avoid a painful reality. Many people have been schooled in the belief that psychological distress of any sort is the result of personal weakness or developmental difficulty. Patients and family members are therefore likely to believe that the patient's psychological pain is a consequence of personality flaws. As a result, they may have a strongly held conviction that the psychological distress must be suffered and mastered without "chemical assistance." Indeed, they may feel that only by correcting shortcomings and deficits *without* medication can the patient demonstrate "moral strength" and thereby "recover" from the illness.

The "moral" view usually places great emphasis on self-reliance and any adjuvant is resisted. Thus, patients and families may object to both medication *and* psychotherapy, regarding them as "crutches" and disapproving of them on that basis. (The use of actual crutches for a broken ankle would be readily accepted by such patients, since their view of physical illness differs greatly from their view of psychological disfunction.)

Some patients and family members with these views will suspect that a clinician who proposes medication as a part of treatment is looking for a quick palliative rather than for a "definitive cure.'' They will view medication as a ''smoke screen'' which obscures conflicts and deficits underlying symptoms while providing only temporary relief and rendering the patient a chronic, dependent invalid. Similarly, the use of anti-psychotic medication for prophylaxis is interpreted by these patients and families as evidence of continuing weakness and failure.

This view of psychotic illness as weakness or flaw in character can have a stubborn persistence despite massive evidence that the disorder is involuntary and disabling. The patient may be made to feel that he is ''spoiled'' and ''self-indulgent'' despite his obvious, desperate attempts to function normally. Therapists who advocate a more tolerant or sympathetic view may be seen by both the patient and his family as ''fuzzy headed,'' that is, morally and intellectually suspect.

Argument about these matters seldom produces useful results. However, the therapist's firm and authoritative statement that the disorder is involuntary and cannot respond to exhortation or threat can at least engage the patient and his family in a discussion of the issue. The therapist can use this opportunity to try to make it clear that while the patient may have personal weaknesses and problems, the psychotic state is an involuntary aspect of the illness which requires medication for its suppression and control. Both the patient and family should be reassured that the patient's efforts and determination will play an important role in his ultimate recovery even though medication will be required to control psychotic symptoms and prevent their recurrence.

When a patient or family have taken a strong ''moral stand'' against the use of medication in the early stages of treatment (or when there is an impasse over any critical treatment issue), it may help to suggest that a consultant be brought in to review the evidence and render a second opinion. This option is often useful for the patient and family, giving them an opportunity to test whether the recommended treatment is a standard and established one. A single therapist can be dismissed as eccentric, but a consultant (especially one chosen by the family) who endorses the treatment may add greatly to the authority of the therapist. Even when another clinician is not actually consulted, the suggestion that patient and family do so may itself be reassuring, since it makes it clear that the clinician is confident enough in his recommendations to subject them to independent review.

Fear of Addiction

A related concern often expressed is a fear of the possible habit-forming or addictive potential of antipsychotic medication. Many patients are aware that some classes of frequently prescribed psychoactive drugs are capable of inducing psychological dependence. A desperate patient may feel such an intense desire for relief from painful symptoms that dependence on medication is feared. This particular concern is relatively easy to deal with. Once the patient acknowledges a fear of dependence or addiction, the therapist can make a strong and direct statement which assures the patient that the medication is not habit-forming. In general, patients are willing to accept as medical fact the therapist's assertion that the medication induces no addition or drug craving. It may be helpful to inform the patient that there is no illicit traffic in these drugs and that they are not used for recreational purposes. While this information may reduce short-term resistance to the medication, it is often insufficient to persuade patients and families that long-term maintenance use of these medications is anything other than a form of dependence akin to drug abuse.

Medication as the Embodiment
of Psychotic Illness

Since the use of antipsychotic medication is concrete evidence that the patient has suffered a major psychiatric illness, it is not remarkable that patients often come to identify the medication with psychosis. For many patients these medications are a concrete manifestation of chronic, massively disabling mental illness. Patients and families may have heard or read about psychiatric patients who are "turned into zombies" through the use of medication which is a "chemical straight jacket." The patient and family may feel a joint determination to avoid this outcome, even if it means doing without or minimizing the use of a recommended treatment. All may insist that the patient, despite severe psychotic symptoms, "is not *that* sick." (If the patient consents to the use of medication, the presence of side effects which make the patient stiff, sedated, and less expressive may accentuate this determination to resist the idea of long-term treatment with antipsychotic medication). The therapist should explore these concerns with the patient, drawing distinctions between degrees of illness. The clinician should maintain that the patient requires the medication while simultaneously reassuring both the patient and family that recovery from the acute episode is to be expected and that a life of chronic disability is not inevitable. Reassurance of this sort often can temporarily overcome this form of resistance to treatment.

Patients are understandably horrified by the possibility of relapse. In struggling with this distress, they often expand and extend the symbolic connection between psychosis and medication until the medication becomes a largely unconscious concrete measure of the severity of their illness and of their vulnerability to relapse. For example, a patient may assume that the higher the dose of medication, the more serious the illness. There is, of course, some rough validity to this idea, since the dose of medication may be raised if a patient's psychotic symptoms worsen. However, patients may take this idea to an irrational extreme. A patient on 25 mg. daily of a given medication may come to see himself as literally one-half as vulnerable to relapse as he was when he was on 50 mg. daily of the same medication. If this idea is carried to its logical conclusion, the patient who is no longer on medication may feel this implies that he is no longer ill and is free of the risk of relapse.

Once a patient becomes invested with this view, he may struggle to have medication reduced, arguing over every milligram, since in his eyes every dosage reduction means that he "is that much less ill." If permitted to continue, the patient may unconsciously view the whole of treatment as the task of convincing the therapist that he is no longer vulnerable to psychotic illness and therefore has no further need of medication. The logic of this approach supposes that if the "expert therapist" can be persuaded to discontinue the medication then the patient is truly no longer vulnerable to psychosis. In the service of this goal patients may unconsciously conceal or minimize difficulties and exaggerate progress.

In addition, if medication is unconsciously thought to embody the illness and the risk of relapse, then the therapist, since he controls the prescription of medication, seems to have the power to keep the patient sick or to make him magically well. Thus, the patient may come to feel he is "ill" only because the therapist insists medication is necessary. As a result, the patient may become suspicious of the therapist's motives and therefore may discount his judgments.

Sometimes the therapist can gradually address these patients' one-sided determination to persuade him that they are invulnerable to relapse. Patients usually have great difficulty with observations of this kind, but carefully timed interpretations can often help them begin to understand that their lack of fear about relapse is a legitimate cause for concern to the therapist. Eventually they may come to realize that the only way to persuade the therapist that they are truly well is to begin to examine the psychotic experience and to confront the reality of possible relapse. In the course of exploration it usually becomes clear that beneath the apparent confidence the patient is extremely frightened of relapse and has great difficulty coping with anxiety about the matter.

Stalemate as a Global Resistance

A patient who has come to see medication as the embodiment of illness may be inaccessible to psychotherapy even if he is compliant with the medication regimen. Effective treatment is impossible if the patient's whole focus is on reduction and discontinuation of medication. If exploratory and interpretive efforts do not succeed, the therapist may eventually be persuaded, against his better judgment, by the patient's efforts and may discontinue medication prematurely, thus permitting the patient to relapse into psychosis. More typically, the therapist will manage to keep the patient on antipsychotic medication but the continuing stalemate in the relationship prevents any useful psychotherapeutic work. Such patients fail to progress beyond the fear of vulnerability to psychosis and the wish that the risk of relapse could be magically and permanently ended.

When the stalemate cannot be broken by exploratory work a different strategy may be necessary. After prolonged stalemate, the therapist can begin to address the fact of an unresolved difference of opinion between the patient and therapist. This impasse can then be approached directly as a serious problem in the treatment. In some instances, the patient will seize this opportunity to suggest that the therapist should resolve the stalemate by allowing the patient to discontinue medication or to reduce the frequency of meetings, or both. The therapist may feel there is no choice but to agree with reluctance. However, in doing so, attempts to negotiate a new treatment agreement with the patient should be made so that these changes can have possible constructive effects on treatment. For example, the therapist might propose a very gradual reduction in medication with an understanding that medication would be resumed, and/or increased, if the patient's symptoms reappeared. If the patient rejects this proposal and insists on discontinuing the medication completely, the clinician can agree reluctantly on the condition that, if the patient should relapse, in subsequent treatment he will cooperate fully with the therapist's recommendations. This strategy provides the clinician with a means to resolve the stalemate in the treatment with a sense of collaboration intact.

The therapist can be candid about the uncertainties involved in these judgments but also can be unequivocal in recommending continuation of medication. This stance has the twin virtues of being truthful and of shifting the disagreement from argument about right and wrong to one about differences in judgments about risks. This approach may permit some patients to continue on medication while clinging to the notion that it is a probably unnecessary deference to an ''overcautious therapist.''

Medication as a Focus for Transference and Countertransference Fantasies

The concrete representation of psychotic illness and of the risk of relapse by no means exhausts the wide range of meanings patients attribute to antipsychotic medication. Medication is tangible, it comes from the therapist, and it has powerful and mysterious actions. This makes medication an especially likely focus for many of the transference fantasies common to any intensive psychotherapy. Problems in compliance with the medication regimen may stem directly from the intrusion of these fantasies into the pharmacologic aspect of the treatment. For example, a patient may unconsciously regard medication as an extension of the therapist and a material representation of the therapist's love and protection. As a result, gradual reduction of the dose of medication and its ultimate discontinuation can be experienced by the patient as a withdrawal by the therapist and may evoke fears of being abandoned. The result may be an upsurge in symptoms and resistance to the reduction in the doses of medication.

Negative transference also may be reflected in the patient's attitudes and behavior regarding medication. For example, some patients may stop taking medication as a means of retaliation against the therapist for some real or imagined rebuff. In other cases, the patient may see medication as evidence of the therapist's intention to ''seduce him into a prolonged dependency.'' A patient may regard the prospect of continued prophylactic treatment with medication as a ploy on the part of the therapist to bind them together indefinitely. Others may see the medication as a form of rejection on the part of the therapist. These patients may experience a prescription of medication as evidence that the therapist cannot tolerate their illness and symptoms and wishes to impose some ''chemical distance'' between them. Paranoid patients may experience medication as a frightening intrusion on the part of the therapist into their consciousness, with a corresponding sense that any change, even an improvement, in the patient's subjective state represents a dangerous loss of control.

Therapists also have unconscious fantasies about medication which may affect their judgments about the use of medication in treatment. The same qualities which make medication a likely focus for the patient's fantasies operate for the therapist as well. For example, a therapist who is becoming anxious about some aspect of a patient's treatment is likely to be tempted to think it can be remedied by a change in the medication regimen. If the therapeutic relationship is tense, angry, frightening, or stagnant, therapists may reduce their distress by defining the matter as an increase in psychotic symptoms and suggesting increase or change in the medication. Unfortunately, this maneuver may succeed in reducing the overt tension and conflict in the therapeutic relationship because of the implied threat of relapse. The therapeutic issue is suppressed indirectly by frightening the patient and suggesting that the tension and arousal in the treatment is a prodromal symptom of psychosis. This maneuver is especially counterproductive, since it makes it more difficult to help the patient differentiate normal and appropriate anger, tension, and emotional arousal from potentially dangerous symptoms. If there are frequent dosage changes or additions of new medications in response to difficulty in the therapeutic relationship, the patient is likely to come to view therapy as simply the quest for the proper combinations and doses of medications. Thus, it is particularly important that the therapist guard against any inclination to use medication for purposes other than for the treatment of acute psychotic symptoms and prophylaxis against relapse. Once a patient has been stabilized on the lowest possible maintenance dose of medication, changes in medication should be infrequent, and the patient should be discouraged from taking extra doses when anxious or upset.

Listening for Covert Meanings

Since medication can be a vehicle for almost any psychotherapeutic issue, the clinician should be alert to covert meanings and be ready to explore them as they arise in treatment. Clinicians who are uncomfortable or evasive with these issues will soon find them intruding in treatment in indirect ways. In fact, much of the dialogue between patient and therapist about medication must be understood in this context. Even when the discussions about medication are open and honest, the patient may use them to raise covert issues. Apparently innocent comments and questions about medication from patients or family members are often unconsciously designed to probe the clinician on associated issues and to test the consistency of his reactions and judgments.

A typical indirect probe might be, for example: "Sometimes I forget to take my medication. Should I take extra doses the next day to catch up?" The clinician should understand that patients often experiment with missing one or more doses of medication and they usually note that no change has taken place. It is important for the clinician to explain that the effect of the medication is cumulative and that harmful effects may not be seen for some time after the medication is reduced or discontinued. Similarly, the patient should also understand that the medication takes at least several weeks to take full effect when treatment is reinstituted. While missing a single dose of medication is unlikely to cause any serious difficulty, the effectiveness of the medication depends on maintaining a consistent and regular dosage.

While providing this factual information, the clinician should keep in mind that the patient is observing carefully to see the degree of concern expressed by the therapist about the missed doses. The patient may be interested in gaining a better understanding of the timing and degree of suddenness of relapse when medication is reduced or discontinued. The possible hidden content of the inquiry might be summarized as: "I know I don't become psychotic when I miss a dose or two of the medication. That makes me think that I am no longer at risk for relapse or at least that I could reduce the dosage of medication. Perhaps you are exaggerating the danger."

A similar issue may be embedded in other apparently off-hand comments. A typical example might be the patient who says lightly, as he rises to leave the office at the end of his session, "Oh, by the way, I'm not sure but I think I may need a renewal of my prescription." As a practical matter the clinician should make sure that the patient leaves with a renewal. The patient should be advised that missing a few days or a week of medication is dangerous because it involves a decrease in protection against relapse. It should be clear to the patient that this increase in risk is of sufficient concern so that extra time will be taken to make sure he does not miss any doses of medication. However, the clinician should be certain to raise the matter in his next session with the patient, suggesting that the patient's uncertainty and casual attitude about the need for a refill suggests that he has questions about the importance of medication, the seriousness of the risk of relapse, and the accuracy of the clinician's judgments. Further exploration may reveal a variety of fears and resentments about the therapist or the treatment which were expressed through the patient's dismissive attitude toward the medication.

Complaints about side effects can also imply similar concerns. For example, a patient may complain: "my vision is so blurred I can't read anything. Can't you do anything about that?" While complaints about side effects should be discussed in detail and every effort made to minimize them whenever possible, the possibility that the complaint is being emphasized because of related underlying questions should also be considered. In this instance the patient may be indirectly asserting "the side effects of medication are interfering with the quality of my life. Do you really think the risk of relapse is so great it justifies subjecting me to this kind of distress? Maybe you just don't care about how much the medication makes me suffer." A direct interpretive statement by the therapist may open the matter for active discussion and exploration of associated transference issues. The result may be a dramatic reduction in complaints about medication side effects, a reduction in the dosage of medication, or both.

Having invited open exploration of these matters in the therapy, the clinician will soon find the patient is pressing for responses to many difficult questions. "How much longer must I take this medication?" "How long must I be in treatment?" "What will happen if I stop taking the medication now?" "Is this medicine doing me any damage now?" "How will we know when I'm ready to stop the medicine?"

All these questions deserve answers. Unfortunately, the therapist is often unable to give definite answers and it is usually wise to avoid giving approximate answers, since patients tend to seize upon approximations and quickly turn them into definitive statements. The best approach for clinicians is to acknowledge their inability to give definite answers and to try to focus the discussion on the problems of balancing risks and benefits. While acknowledging the risks and side effects associated with treatment with antipsychotic medication, clinicians can reaffirm their judgment that the benefits outweigh the risks. If it is early in the course of the patient's convalescence, the clinician can stress that it is too early to begin considering these questions and can suggest that prudence demands that changes in treatment be deferred. Depending on the assessment of the patient's vulnerability to relapse, the therapist can suggest a time when the questions might be more appropriately raised for more extensive discussion.

It is also helpful if clinicians stress their commitment to conservative management, since patients, at times, insist they are willing to accept substantial risks to avoid continuing treatment with medication. By stressing the need to keep risk to an absolute minimum, the clinician may avoid appearing to be continually threatening the patient with relapse. Ultimately, the answers to these questions are best arrived at jointly, near the end of convalescence, as part of an overall treatment strategy.

CHAPTER VII

When the Therapist Is Not a Physician

A GREAT MANY of the therapists who treat outpatients suffering from psychotic disorders are not psychiatrists and cannot prescribe medication. The need for clinicians skilled in treating these patients is so great that psychiatrists alone cannot begin to meet the demand. Consequently, despite the fact that medication is a central part of the treatment of these patients, large numbers of therapists who are not physicians (social workers, psychologists, nurse-clinicians and others) successfully manage and treat patients with psychotic disorders, relying on a psychiatrist to provide necessary medication and supervise its administration. In these circumstances, therapists who are not physicians must deal constantly with medication-related issues without either the formal training or the legal authority required to prescribe medication and with clinical responsibility shared between two clinicians with different training and differing relationships with the patient. Psychotic patients are difficult to treat under the best of circumstances, and the introduction of a second clinician compounds that difficulty. Despite (or perhaps because of) this difficulty, no generally accepted guidelines or procedures have been developed to help clinicians structure this shared responsibility.

Non-MD Clinicians and Psychiatrists:
Informal Arrangements

In most instances the relationship between the two clinicians evolves informally as the two work together with a variety of patients. At times the administrative structure of a clinic setting or the practical needs of one or both clinicians shapes the working relationship and the structure of the treatment. In practice the result is a wide variety of informal solutions to the problem of shared responsibility; solutions which vary in their effectiveness. Within the limits of what is possible and practical, these informal solutions attempt to meet the requirements of medicine and law regarding the prescription of medication while maintaining the focus of treatment on the larger psychotherapeutic tasks.

Some of these informally developed solutions to shared responsibility are clearly defective. The worst of these models are those attempting to minimize the difficulties or to ignore them. For example, in some cases the therapist tries to behave like a prescribing physician, altering doses of medication and discussing medical risks and side effects with patients under the "supervision" of a psychiatrist who actually signs the prescriptions. In some institutions the therapist actually makes out the prescription forms which are then signed by a psychiatrist who may or may not have seen the patient. In many cases this may seem a practical solution to the problem, since the psychiatrist may be available on a very limited basis and nonphysician therapists often have considerable clinical experience with the use of antipsychotic medication and may know a great deal about how it is prescribed.

While arrangements of this sort effectively minimize the role of the psychiatrist and thus eliminate most of the problems of a divided treatment, they do so at considerable cost. Aside from the obvious medical–legal difficulties generated when a therapist without medical training makes pharmacologic decisions, this sort of lopsided solution to the problem of divided treatment often leads to major psychotherapeutic difficulties as well. Patients in this kind of treatment arrangement are inevitably troubled by the perception that the nonphysician therapist is "bending the rules" and acting outside his proper authority. Therapists sometimes persuade themselves that patients are ignorant of or indifferent to these matters, but patients almost always care deeply and the awareness that there is something "improper" in the clinician's behavior can have an adverse effect on the therapeutic alliance.

A clinician should keep in mind that the effectiveness of psychotherapy always depends on the patient's conviction that the therapist is fully trustworthy. A therapist who exercises authority beyond the scope of his training may compromise his integrity in the eyes of his patient. A few patients may have the courage to ask "are you supposed to be in charge of my medication?" and the therapist will be hard put to give a convincing answer. Unfortunately, most patients have great difficulty in raising questions of this sort, but the patient's silence on these matters should not be construed as approval. Even when patients deny concern about nonphysician therapists taking responsibility for prescribing and monitoring medication, they may conclude that psychotropic medication differs from other medication in that it appears that medical training is unnecessary to administer it properly. It is easy for the patient to reason subsequently that since nonphysicians can make expert decisions about these medications, patients can also make independent decisions about psychopharmacologic treatment.

It is easy to underestimate the importance of a patient's trust in the therapist's integrity and expertise. Each patient should feel certain that his clinician will take care not to exceed the limits of his authority in any sphere. Differences of opinion between clinicians and patients about treatment issues are common, especially about antipsychotic medications. Successful resolution of these differences of opinion must evolve from an interchange between patients and clinicians, often ultimately depending on patients' trust in the disciplined expertise of their clinicians. It is therefore essential that the nonphysician therapist carefully define the limits of his authority. Treatment in which a nonphysician therapist behaves like a prescribing psychiatrist is not merely bad medicine, but also bad psychotherapy.

Another common and equally defective model which attempts to solve the problem of divided clinical responsibility involves the formal division of treatment into two distinct segments—psychotherapeutic and psychopharmacologic. This kind of arrangement relegates the prescription of medication and discussions about medication to a psychiatrist while the therapist talks with the patient only about issues other than medication. This model conceives of discussions about medication in the psychotherapeutic portion of treatment as defensive diversions from more important psychotherapeutic work. Consequently, the patient is instructed to discuss with the psychiatrist any questions or concerns about medication. Given the importance of covert issues which are expressed in concerns and questions about medication, this kind of arrangement is likely to compromise psychotherapeutic work. The exploration of covert meanings of medication, an essential part of the assessment of the patient's vulnerability to relapse, becomes fragmented and obscured as a consequence. At its worst, this bifurcation of the treatment may land the patient in two essentially separate and possibly conflicting treatments.

Fortunately, most clinicians avoid these simplistic extremes and find some intermediate stance, viewing treatment as an informal collaboration between the therapist and the psychiatrist with considerable overlap in their joint treatment responsibility. When both clinicians share similar treatment philosophies and have an established working relationship, questions the patient raises about the use and risks of medication and about vulnerability to relapse can be handled by both clinicians with a mutual sense that their efforts are complementary. When two clinicians have a good working relationship, they can often sense when their efforts are beginning to diverge in emphasis and direction. By staying in frequent contact and fully discussing these matters they can usually correct problems before they cause serious disruption of the treatment.

Structuring a Divided Treatment

Clinicians can avoid most difficulties by clearly having in mind some basic principles and operational ground rules for structuring a divided treatment. Perhaps the most important of these principles is that there be a clearly defined primary clinician who is seen by all parties to be in charge of the treatment. In this situation the therapist must be the primary clinician and the psychiatrist must be a collaborating specialist. In fact, the psychiatrist's role is a complex combination of the roles of consultant and co-therapist. This is not a simple matter, since the treatment responsibilities of both clinicians overlap to some degree and decisions specifically involving medication must be made by the psychiatrist.

The psychiatrist must confirm the diagnosis of a psychotic disorder. It is that diagnosis which forms the basis for treatment with antipsychotic medication. The psychiatrist is then responsible for prescribing the medication and for monitoring dosage, side effects, and the patient's clinical response. The psychiatrist must weigh the medical risks and benefits of treatment with antipsychotic medication and educate the patient in order to obtain informed consent.

The primary clinician has sole responsibility for psychotherapeutic work with patients on their attitudes and response to illness, ideas of vulnerability to relapse, and on maladaptive patterns of behavior and limitations in functional capacity. Thus, many issues can be defined as belonging exclusively in the domain of one or the other clinician.

However, patients' attitudes towards treatment with medication and problems in compliance with a treatment regimen are matters which fall to the two clinicians' overlapping responsibilities. The patient's fantasies, concerns, and questions about medication usually address simultaneously both medical and psychotherapeutic aspects of the role of medication, especially with regard to the patient's attitude toward and concerns about the need for continuing prophylaxis against recurrent psychosis. Patients may have realistic concerns and questions about the uses, risks, and side effects of medication. Questions of this sort are properly handled by the collaborating psychiatrist. However, concerns about medication are often a device through which the patient can focus and express a great many related therapeutic concerns. The therapeutic issues raised by these concerns should be dealt with in the context of the psychotherapy which is conducted by the primary clinician.

It is this overlapping area that must be managed collaboratively by the two clinicians so that the practical details of medication management and the psychotherapeutic meanings of medication can be approached simultaneously without ignoring their complexity and without confusing the patient. This collaboration is possible only if both clinicians are sensitive to the rich variety of meanings inherent in the patient's concerns about medication and if each takes care not to intrude into the therapeutic province of the other. Each, in turn, must be sufficiently knowledgeable so that he or she can keep the other properly informed. The primary clinician should be able to discuss medication knowledgeably with the patient and understand indications, typical actions, possible risks, and complications. Yet, it is important that the primary clinician not act like a prescribing psychiatrist, but rather coordinate psychotherapeutic work about the uses and meanings of medication with the collaborating psychiatrist. Similarly, while alert to the complex meanings of the patient's concerns about medication, the psychiatrist should take care to refer these psychotherapeutic matters back to the primary clinician.

Much depends on the close collaboration between primary clinician and psychiatrist while dealing with medication use and its implications. It is particularly important that the primary clinician and the psychiatrist have similar assessments of the patient's vulnerability to recurrent psychosis and of the need for prophylactic treatment with antipsychotic medication. Major differences of opinion or philosophy between the two clinicians on these matters can have catastrophic results for the treatment. Even comparatively minor differences of opinion between the two clinicians can cause considerable difficulty, since they may come to assume an exaggerated importance for the patient.

Both clinicians should bear in mind that it is the primary clinician who negotiates each aspect of the patient's treatment agreement. Thus, the psychiatrist should take care not to undermine the authority of the primary clinician by making major treatment decisions during brief meetings with the patient. Any major decision about medication which is not an immediate medical necessity should be made only after it is clear that the psychiatrist has consulted with the primary clinician, either privately or with the patient present. While minor adjustment in the dosage of medication can be made independently by the psychiatrist, major changes such as significant reduction in dosage or discontinuing medication should clearly be joint decisions.

Trouble is least likely to occur if the primary therapist can be present when the psychiatrist meets with the patient. This is especially true for the initial meetings of psychiatrist and patient, particularly if the patient is at all hesitant or fearful about taking medication. The presence of both clinicians is the most direct and simple way to avoid difficulties stemming from a divided treatment; it makes it fully clear to the patient that the two clinicians are working in a direct and mutually respectful collaboration. The presence of both clinicians avoids the possibility of separate and conflicting dialogues developing between the patient and each clinician. The two clinicians can jointly handle questions about vulnerability to psychosis, about the implications of treatment with medication, and about the duration of treatment with medication with a minimum of misunderstanding and confusion. The presence of both clinicians also makes it possible to address medical questions and underlying psychotherapeutic issues in the same session while keeping clear about the boundaries between the responsibilities of the two clinicians. Fantasies about the relationship between the two clinicians are less likely to arise, since the patient has the opportunity to observe directly how the clinicians exchange information and jointly arrive at decisions and recommendations.

Unfortunately, the practical realities of the structure of both private practice and clinic settings often make the joint presence of both clinicians at these meetings difficult or impossible. A variety of compromise arrangements can be nearly as satisfactory. For example, if both clinicians can be present for the initial meetings and occasionally thereafter, most difficulties can be avoided. Where the two clinicians cannot be present together at all, or only very rarely, regular conversations between them, especially before each of the patient's meetings with the psychiatrist, is a less satisfactory, but still workable, alternative. At the very least, the two clinicians should meet together with the patient when any problem has developed in their collaboration or where the patient suggests a major discrepancy in the advice received from them.

Unless the matter is an urgent one, the primary clinician and psychiatrist should discuss a proposed change in medication either in the presence of the patient or in private before broaching the subject with the patient. This procedure helps the patient to have a continuing sense that the primary clinician is in charge and that although medication is an essential part of the treatment regimen, the role of the psychiatrist is that of a consultant-collaborator with limited and carefully defined responsibility.

From the outset it is the primary clinician who negotiates the treatment conditions with the patient, making the initial suggestion to the patient that medication is a possibility in treatment and explaining the referral to the psychiatrist for medication assessment. In general, it is poor practice to refer an outpatient who is reluctant to take medication to the psychiatrist in hopes that he will persuade the patient where the primary clinician has failed. This tactic conveys the unfortunate impression to patients that since they are not sufficiently cooperative, they are being sent to a ''higher authority'' who will try to extract agreement from them. Whatever the outcome, the patient may easily form the impression that the primary clinician is "junior member" of the treatment team.

However, on occasion it may be useful to refer a patient to the psychiatrist if he is hesitant or doubtful about medication. The psychiatrist should be advised that this is the case and that the patient is being referred to provide an opportunity to meet the psychiatrist, to discuss concerns about medication, and to reduce anxieties about dealing with a second clinician. It also gives the psychiatrist an opportunity to assess the patient and to confirm the primary clinician's impression that medication is indicated.

Successful collaboration between the two clinicians requires that each provide essential information to the other on a regular basis. The primary clinician should inform the psychiatrist about the patient's progress in treatment, about changes in target symptoms expected to respond to treatment with medication, possible side effects, and problems in the patient's attitude or concern about medication. The psychiatrist, in turn, should inform the primary clinician of the patient's clinical response to medication, observed side effects, and any proposed changes in dosage. Any questions or issues raised by the patient concerning vulnerability to relapse or the likely duration of treatment with medication should be deferred until the psychiatrist and primary clinician have had the opportunity to confer. Since both clinicians can safely assume that any question on these subjects will be asked separately of both clinicians, it is important that both respond with a single, jointly agreed upon, answer. When the two clinicians differ in their opinions as to fundamental questions about treatment with medication, the differences must be resolved so that both can present a united front to the patient. One or both clinicians may have to modify his views to make a coherent treatment possible. If major differences cannot be resolved, the two clinicians should stop working together.

In some instances the psychiatrist who is collaborating with the primary clinician may also be functioning as supervisor for that clinician, an arrangement in training settings which can cause significant difficulties in the treatment if it is not handled carefully. In this instance the psychiatrist is a collaborator, a consultant, as well as a supervisor and superior, for the primary clinician in the same treatment. Such a complicated arrangement can work only if the psychiatrist is especially alert to the complexities of his role and to the therapist's need to feel and be seen to be in charge of the treatment.

Divided Transference

The difficulties of conducting a psychotherapeutic treatment in which two clinicians share responsibility for a single patient is best understood as a series of dilemmas resulting from the fact that the patient's transference is divided. Effective psychotherapy is wholly dependent on an evolving relationship between patient and therapist, a relationship which comes to embody "transferred" aspects of earlier relationships in the patient's life. The conscious and unconscious projection of early feeling states and fantasies onto the therapist can suffer disturbing divisions when patients are involved with two clinicians responsible for their care. The result can be serious complications and disruptions in the treatment. Since medication is the issue which ties the two clinicians together and which defines the overlap in their clinical responsibilities, difficulties caused by divided transference are most likely to be expressed in problems involving the use of medication.

Divided transference may permit a patient to project a wide variety of differences on the two clinicians. The patient may conceptualize the clinicians as superior and subordinate, good and bad, competent and incompetent, loving and hateful, weak and strong, or the like. In many instances the patient may recreate aspects of relations with parents, exaggerating small differences between the clinicians, especially if one clinician is male and the other female.

A particularly common division of transference may take the form of elaborated fantasies on the part of the patient about differences in status and training between the two clinicians. The patient may come to see the primary clinician as inferior because of less extensive or prestigious training than that of the psychiatrist. As a result, patients may fantasize that the primary clinician is a trainee or subordinate responsible to the psychiatrist. They may imagine that the work with the primary clinician is being ''checked'' or ''corrected'' by the psychiatrist. If the two clinicians have difficulty with issues of status and training between them, the patient may be subtly encouraged to elaborate this fantasy with a destructive effect on the treatment. When one clinician feels superior to the other (or if one clinician feels inferior), this division of transference can take hold and sabotage the treatment.

Once a division of this sort has been established, patients generally have a mixed reaction. They often feel sympathetic and protective toward the primary clinician, but they can also be disappointed and contemptuous. The patient may therefore be reluctant to complain about medication or to discuss poor compliance with a medication regimen for fear that this information would reflect badly on the performance of the primary clinician and ''get him into trouble.'' Alternatively, if patients become angry or dissatisfied with the therapist, they may refuse medication or complain bitterly about it as a way of ''punishing and embarrassing'' their primary clinician in the eyes of the imagined ''superior.''

Patients are often quite curious about the relationship between the two clinicians and will inquire about it directly and indirectly until they have a conception of how the two clinicians work together or until they are actively discouraged from pursuing further exploration. Both clinicians should be prepared to answer questions about their relationship which the patient poses directly or indirectly. For example, the primary clinician should expect to be asked: ''Is the doctor your boss?'' Or more indirectly, ''Social workers only go to school for two years, isn't that so?'' Or ''Psychiatrists earn a great deal more money than psychologists, don't they?'' Answers to these sorts of questions must be simple, straightforward, and scrupulously honest. Primary clinicians must be candid about their training experience and level of expertise without being defensive or apologetic.

At the same time, the primary clinician can use the opportunity to educate the patient about the role of the psychiatrist and explore the patient's fantasies regarding the relationship of the two clinicians. Thus, the therapist may say: "The psychiatrist has specialized and detailed training about the medical aspects of medication and I rely on his advice about its use. However, I am in charge of your treatment and make the overall decisions about your care." Primary clinicians should take care to avoid minimizing or disparaging the importance of the psychiatrist. For example, they should not imply that the psychiatrist is really unnecessary and is involved only because there is a legal necessity that a physician prescribe medication.

The patient may come to see one clinician as "the good therapist" and the other as "the bad therapist." In this form of invariably destructive, divided transference "the good therapist" is seen as unfailingly understanding, sympathetic, helpful, and wise. In contrast, "the bad therapist" is invariably insensitive, tactless, of doubtful competence, and often malicious. The patient may consume considerable time in discussing the merits or deficits of the "other clinician" during meetings with each, deflecting the work from its appropriate content. This kind of division flourishes when it plays on feelings and concerns shared covertly by one or both clinicians.

When a clinician detects a development of this sort, prompt action is required. The split must be addressed directly with the patient and, in particular, the negative side of the division should be confronted. Each clinician should consistently respond to the patient's excessive praise or criticism of his colleague by observing that these exaggerated comments have become a pattern which is interfering with the progress of treatment. The patient should be encouraged to discuss affectionate or hostile feelings directly with the clinician at whom they are directed. It is also useful to inform the patient that the two clinicians work as a team and that if the patient wishes to change one of the clinicians he must necessarily change both.

Both clinicians should examine their behavior to determine whether they indirectly encouraged and fostered the "good versus bad" split. For example, when the patient has identified the psychiatrist as the "bad therapist," unexpressed differences of opinion between the clinicians concerning the use of medication may have led to subtle encouragement of the patient's hostility towards the use of medication and thus towards the psychiatrist who prescribes it. In instances where the patient is reluctant to take medication, the primary clinician may be attempting to deflect the patient's anger by suggesting that medication continues only at the psychiatrist's insistence. When the patient has labeled the primary clinician the "bad therapist," it is especially urgent that the patient's concerns and criticisms be actively explored both within the treatment and between the two clinicians. This situation usually results from serious problems in the alliance between patient and primary clinician, and may not stem directly from aspects of divided transference. However, in some instances unexpressed differences of opinion between the two clinicians concerning the conduct of the psychotherapy may have been communicated to the patient, enhancing distrust of the primary clinician. It is absolutely essential that the two clinicians resolve differences of this sort, since this kind of split in the transference threatens the integrity of the treatment.

Much depends on regular and thoughtful communication between the two clinicians. If they can work together with tact and mutual respect, particularly in the areas where their tasks overlap, few difficulties are likely to arise. The necessary communication between the clinicians requires time and effort, but it is only by making that effort that the difficulties of a divided treatment can be overcome.

CHAPTER VIII

The End of Convalescence

CONVALESCENCE FROM PSYCHOTIC ILLNESS is usually character-ized by slow, uneven progress. After a period of from four months to a year or more following the acute psychotic epi-sode, a patient's rate of progress in treatment slows as he ap-proaches premorbid levels of function. For some patients the end of convalescence means the recovery of all premorbid ca-pacities and these patients can resume their lives free of resid-ual symptoms or deficits. Other patients, particularly those who have suffered multiple psychotic episodes, may reach the end of convalescence and fall well short of their premorbid ca-pacities. In any case, the overall rate of symptomatic improve-ment for all patients slows progressively until they eventually reach a "plateau" at which symptoms and level of function re-main relatively constant.

Since convalescence ends gradually, there is no clear-cut clinical event which marks the transition to the post-convales-cent period. Patients have a wide variety of reactions as they become aware that they are approaching the end of their con-valescence. Many patients report that they once again regard themselves as "normal" or "recovered." Some even report that they feel stronger than ever before. In some cases the therapist will agree, but often he has a distinctly different assessment. Some patients, often, but not always, those with histories of recurrent psychotic illness, are keenly disappointed at their residual deficits and they may become demoralized as a result of difficulties which continue into the post-convalescent period.

Patients' Questions

Whatever the mixture of progress and deficit, relief and disappointment, patients approaching the end of convalescence begin to raise questions about the purpose and direction of future treatment. For most patients medication has been lowered to maintenance levels months earlier, reducing troublesome side effect to a minimum. The patient usually has been able to function in a reasonably stable way at school, at work, or in a structured treatment program designed to meet the patient's special needs. A substantial period of time has elapsed since the acute psychotic episode and fears of relapse, though still present, have been tempered by the passage of time.

It is at this juncture that the therapeutic work of the convalescent period is gradually put to the test. In particular, any unresolved differences between the patient and therapist regarding vulnerability to relapse now become central factors in determining future treatment. The discussions and explorations of the convalescent period now must be somehow translated into a new treatment plan which ideally reflects a collaborative strategy for the future. In arriving at this strategy both the patient and therapist must now address some basic questions. Should the patient's medication be discontinued? Should medication be used intermittently when the patient's symptoms require it? How quickly can medication be discontinued? How much supervision of the patient is required while medications are being discontinued? Does the patient wish to continue psychotherapy? What would be the goals of continuing psychotherapeutic treatment? If the patient has no particular psychotherapeutic goals he wishes to pursue, must he continue to see a therapist?

Redefining the Roles of Medication and Psychotherapy

The answers to these questions must emerge from the dialogue that has been developing between patient and therapist over the whole of their previous relationship. For some patients the need for continued treatment with medication is obvious. Those whose history is marked by repeated psychotic episodes, disabling residual psychotic symptoms, or difficulty in collaborating to prevent relapse are likely to need continuing treatment with prophylactic medication. Many of these patients will need to take medication indefinitely, although some can learn eventually to use medication on an intermittent basis. Even when the need for continuous treatment with medication is apparent to both patient and therapist, both must still decide whether continued psychotherapeutic treatment is indicated and, if so, what might be the goals of such treatment.

For patients who do not clearly require continuous treatment with prophylactic medication, a plan must be devised which gradually defines the roles of medication and psychotherapy after convalescence. In a practical sense, this usually means that the patient feels increasingly ready to cope with the risk of relapse and begins to press the clinician to define conditions under which it would be safe to decrease (and ultimately discontinue) medication. In responding, the clinician must be candid with the patient that the process is inevitably one of trial and error and that any strategy represents a clinical judgment which attempts to balance risks and benefits. If the therapeutic alliance is a good one and the patient and therapist generally agree about vulnerability, it is usually possible to jointly define conditions under which it is possible to begin the process of decreasing medication.

When Should Medication Be Discontinued?

While any given set of clinical conditions for discontinuing medication must be tailored to the needs and vulnerabilities of each individual patient, some general guidelines are worth noting. Before reducing medication below established maintenance levels, it must be clear that the patient has been clinically stable for a reasonable period of time. Having returned to or near to premorbid status, the patient should be able to function reasonably well at work, at school, or in a structured rehabilitation program. His life should be free of any serious turmoil or distress. Symptoms should be absent or relatively mild and infrequent, while overtly psychotic symptoms should be absent altogether.

The patient should not be facing any major life changes or stresses in the immediate future. Since the life of every human being is filled with change and stress, the clinician cannot insist on a period of perfect tranquility. However, a patient who is about to begin a new job, to return to college, to graduate from college, to begin his first serious love affair, or to leave home for the first time is *not* a suitable candidate for decrease in dosage of medication. These may seem obvious points, but it is often just at these times of major change that patients press most strongly to discontinue medication (and often to discontinue treatment altogether). The wish to "start a new life" and leave reminders of the psychotic illness behind is strongest when the patient is about to embark on a major life change. The therapist should take the position that the time to begin reducing the dose of medication is after the patient has made the change and after it is clear that he has managed that change in a secure and stable way. Prudence, not pessimism, dictates that the "experiment" with decreasing the patient's protection against relapse be conducted in a context which minimizes risks and offers every possible opportunity to abort an impending relapse should that prove necessary.

Techniques for Discontinuing Medication

Unless there is some pressing reason to do otherwise, only one medication should be changed at a time. When the patient is on more than one medication, the process of lowering and finally discontinuing a given medication should be completed before beginning to decrease the dosage of a second medication, making it possible for the clinician to understand the effect of each change in medication dosage. In general, antidepressants usually should be tapered first and discontinued entirely before antipsychotic medications are tapered at all, since antidepressants may activate psychotic symptoms in some patients who are not taking antipsychotics. Also, in patients with bipolar disorders neuroleptic medications should be tapered and discontinued before lithium dosage is altered since many of these patients will require long-term prophylaxis with lithium alone. These are obviously not rigid requirements, but they are useful guidelines for the clinician in attempting to keep the process of reducing medication intelligible and under control. Of course, on occasion clinical circumstances may warrant a different order of medication reduction.

The clinician should determine not only that the patient is doing well enough clinically to warrant decreasing the dose of medication. The clinician should also be clear that the patient is properly prepared psychotherapeutically to cope with the risks which the process entails. The patient should understand clearly that the process is one of trial and error and that careful observation of his clinical response is the only way to determine whether a given decrease in the dose of medication is workable. The patient should be a collaborator who is willing to reverse the process and increase the medication should that prove necessary.

It is usually best to present to the patient each change in dosage as a distinct and separate clinical trial. That is to say, the clinician should not suggest that "we can now begin to discontinue your medication." Rather, he should suggest that it is time to attempt a modest reduction in the dosage. It should be made clear to the patient that once the dosage is reduced the new dosage will remain constant for a period of time to ensure that any effects of the reduction can be observed carefully to be certain that there is no recurrence of symptoms. Once it is clear that the patient has tolerated the reduction of medication well, a second reduction can be proposed. In this manner medication can be reduced in a series of separate and controlled steps. The time required to discontinue the medication gives both the clinician and the patient an ample period to observe any adverse effects resulting from each change. Each separate step gives the clinician the opportunity to review with the patient possible symptoms and problems which might develop as a result of the reduction and to be certain that the patient understands the risks involved.

The patient should be reminded that it may be necessary to raise the dose of medication back to its original level (or even temporarily above the original level) if signs of relapse should appear. Should it be necessary to reverse the process and raise the dose of medication due to recurrent symptoms, the patient can be reassured that the process of reducing medication can be resumed at a later date. All of this advance discussion and effort is essential, since patients at the end of convalescence are usually far more willing to decrease the dosage of medication than to increase it, even when the increase is clearly necessary. On the other hand, no matter how confident he may be, nearly every patient has some understanding that each reduction in the dose of medication leads to some increase in the risk of relapse. Thus, the process usually generates considerable anxiety in the patient and the clinician must take this into account. The technique of making each reduction a discrete step helps to control anxiety and the successful negotiation of each step in the tapering process helps to reassure the patient of his safety. If psychotic symptoms begin to recur, it is usually easier to help a patient accept the need to increase the dosage if he has not been led to expect that the medication would soon be discontinued altogether.

Discontinuing medication can evoke the same range of fantasies and reactions characteristic of earlier phases of treatment. Unconscious meanings attributed to the medication can distort the process of decreasing it and disrupt the treatment. For example, a patient who views the medication as an extension of the therapist may experience a decrease in dosage as a withdrawal or rejection by the therapist and respond with increased symptoms or dependency. On the other hand, patients who have come to equate medication with illness and relapse will tend to be excessively encouraged by each decrease in dosage and may minimize any associated symptoms or problems. The clinician should use the intervals between changes in dosage to explore these and related reactions and fantasies so that the patient can be helped to remain a useful collaborator in this critical phase of treatment.

Discontinuing Medication for Patients with Bipolar Disorders

Patients with schizoaffective or bipolar disorders usually should remain medicated with lithium for a minimum of several years after their first psychotic episode. Indeed, most adolescents and young adults with these disorders require both lithium *and* a neuroleptic agent for a minimum of several years. Perhaps the majority of these patients will require continuous treatment with lithium and at least intermittent treatment with neuroleptics until they reach their mid-to-late 20s. At that time the antipsychotic medication can often be discontinued altogether. Many of these patients, particularly those who have suffered two or more episodes of psychosis, will require indefinite prophylaxis with lithium.

Protecting Patients Who Relapse

While some patients are able to discontinue medication and never have any further psychotic experience, other suffer recurrent psychosis weeks, months, or occasionally years after medication is reduced or discontinued altogether. For those who will relapse, control of this vulnerability depends on the patient's and/or family member's capacity, independently and in collaboration with the therapist, to identify prodromal symptoms of psychosis and to institute appropriate treatment with antipsychotic medication before the occurence of a full-blown psychotic episode. The effort expended during the convalescent period in exploring and carefully noting the details of earlier prodromal periods can help to provide the patient with a foundation of knowledge and understanding necessary if he is to control his vulnerability with intermittent use of medication.

Prodromal Symptoms of Psychosis

After a first psychotic episode patients and their families are often under the impression that the psychosis began suddenly. In fact this is rarely the case. The onset of psychotic symptoms is preceded by a prodromal phase of illness of variable length. A majority of patients who suffer recurrent psychotic episodes decompensate following a prodromal syndrome which is similar in many ways to earlier prodromal experiences. In fact, the similarities in each patient's successive prodromal experiences are great enough so that many patients and family members can learn to recognize one or more telltale prodromal symptoms with considerable accuracy. The early recognition of prodromal symptoms makes it possible for many patients and/or family members to act quickly to abort an impending psychotic episode through the intermittent use of antipsychotic medication.

Prodromal symptoms vary widely in nature and duration. In some patients the onset of prodromal symptoms escalates rapidly, with full-blown psychotic symptoms developing within a few days or less. In other patients an insidiously progressive prodromal syndrome develops over a considerably longer period of time, shading gradually into frank psychotic symptoms. Only by a careful review of the patient's history, discussions with family members, and through repeated exploratory efforts can the details of a particular patient's experience be defined.

The very earliest signs of decompensation are often a sense of an increased alertness, energy, and well-being. In some cases this may be because the patient has discontinued medication and is no longer suffering from uncomfortable side effects. In patients with bipolar disorders, an incipient manic episode often begins with "improvement" which progresses through hypomania to frank manic psychosis. In other patients a brief period of "improvement" is soon followed by a period of increasing anxiety, tension, and preoccupation. The anxiety often increases steadily in intensity and is often accompanied by gradually increasing agitation and a sense of foreboding.

Sleep disturbance is an especially common prodromal symptom. Other symptoms can include marked ideas of reference, depressive symptoms, depersonalization, and an urgent sense that some effort must be made to change or improve. Patients occasionally begin intense programs of self-improvement, such as rigorous exercise, dieting, weight lifting, giving up cigarettes, or the like. Increased drug use may also be a part of a prepsychotic syndrome as patients attempt to relieve their growing distress. The drugs may make the patient feel worse, but their use may continue nonetheless since the patient, in desperation, refuses to recognize that the drugs have lost their capacity to provide relief. In fact, drug use often accelerates the development of psychotic symptoms and may shorten the prodromal period considerably. In some instances a period of intense and prolonged drug use or the use of hallucinogenic agents such as LSD or PCP can precipitate a psychotic episode with little in the way of definable prodromal symptoms.

Gradually increasing suspiciousness and progressive social withdrawal are also common in the early prodromal phases. As prodromal symptoms progress and worsen, perceptual distortions with visual or auditory *illusions* may occur. Patients often report a sense that the world is somehow strange or different and they may experience a vague sense of dread or a conviction that something terrible is about to happen. They may be preoccupied with fears of losing control or "going crazy." The prepsychotic patient often reports a sense that the world is becoming "strange" or "uncanny." Objects and events seem charged with ill-defined, but especially intense, significance. Daily activities often have a "timeless" quality which make them seem somehow extraordinary. As the patient becomes overtly psychotic he may begin to feel that objects and events are charged with meaning that applies specifically to him and that personal messages can be detected in what would otherwise be considered random objects or occurrences. Changes in appetite and emotional lability may also be part of the prepsychotic symptom picture.

A particularly common early prodromal symptom is difficulty in concentration. It usually begins as difficulty with sustained concentration on tasks which require intellectual effort, the sort of difficulty that everyone suffers from time to time. As the symptom worsens it progresses into an inability to maintain attention on even usually pleasant tasks. The intrusion of obsessional thoughts or simply the inability to ignore distracting stimuli make the effort required for concentration painfully demanding. Eventually the patient may experience "periods of abstraction" when he is absorbed in ruminations or his attention is diverted from the task he is pursuing. This is often most apparent in conversation when patients discover they are unable to follow the thread of a conversation and frequently "tune out" and miss much of what is said. Eventually friends and acquaintances begin to notice and often will express concern about the patient's difficulty.

For some patients a prominent prodromal symptom is a preoccupation with a particular idea or concern. The content may be suspicious or grandiose, pleasureable or frightening, vague or highly specific. For example, a patient may feel increasingly convinced of his great intelligence or talent. He may feel that he is on the verge of a great discovery or invention. Obsessive doubts and preoccupations, often focused on sexual or religious themes, may also become prominent. Patients may become fearful of attack or become preoccupied with concerns about homosexuality. Depressive symptoms with accompanying social withdrawal and neurovegetative changes may also be part of the prodromal picture. On occasion suicidal ideation and sometimes suicidal gestures or attempts may become a particularly dangerous aspect of the prodromal experience.

As the prodromal symptoms intensify the patient may experience a growing fear of losing control which can escalate into an agitated, panicky state. For some patients, particularly those who have already experienced a psychotic episode, this panic may crystalize around a fear of psychosis. Having recognized prodromal symptoms of psychosis, the patient may experience a terror which spirals rapidly out of control and accelerates the onset of frank psychotic symptoms.

Exploring Prodromal Symptoms

If a patient is to be able to discontinue medications safely, he should be able to recognize early symptoms of recurrent psychosis (either independently or with the aid of his clinician) and institute appropriate treatment with antipsychotic medication. He must be able to avoid panic and maintain judgment and control while identifying the risk of impending psychosis. This difficult task is possible only if the therapeutic alliance is a strong one and the patient has explored his prepsychotic experience so that he is properly prepared to recognize prodromal symptoms and take appropriate action. Exploration of the prepsychotic experience involves more than simply describing prodromal symptoms. There is little to be gained by providing the patient with a list of typical prodromal symptoms. The clinician may be tempted to ask the patient a series of questions designed to elicit information about his prepsychotic experience. This may provide the therapist with some useful information and make it possible for the patient to summarize his prodromal symptoms. However, this exercise has little value for the patient when it comes to recognizing prodromal symptoms when they actually occur.

A careful and repeated exploratory effort is required, one which reconstructs the content of the patient's prodromal experience, making it possible for prodromal symptoms to be recognized at the time they recur. For example, it is useless to have the patient report that he had "difficulty with concentration" in the weeks prior to his psychotic episode. Instead the patient should be encouraged to recall as many instances of disturbed concentration as he can, describing the details of the experience and reconstructing his impressions and reactions to the symptom. In instances where other people noted his difficulty with concentration, his initial reaction to their observations should also be explored.

Similarly, it is of little use for the patient to simply note that sleep disturbance was an important prodromal symptom for him. What might be useful, for example, is the clear recollection that he remained awake and preoccupied for several days during his prodromal period, that he was so deeply preoccupied that he hardly noticed that he had not slept, and that there were particular feelings, concerns, and perceptions associated with those sleepless nights. In other cases it might be useful to determine whether the patient was worried about his sleep disturbance. Did he take sleep medication? Did he lie restlessly in bed trying to sleep or was he up and active all night? The more the unique quality of the experience is repeatedly spelled out in detail, the more likely it is to be of use in identifying a future prodromal experience.

In the course of this exploration it may become apparent that the patient is able to think clearly about only some of his prodromal symptoms, while others are particularly difficult to explore. In such cases it is best to focus on those symptoms that the patient is able to explore, even if they are not the earliest or most prominent. For some patients the prodromal experience provides a wide variety of symptoms which can be usefully identified and explored. In other cases the particular constellation of prodromal symptoms offers only limited opportunities for exploratory effort.

> Scott is a 19-year-old single man whose difficulties began approximately six months prior to his hospitalization and shortly after he began the second semester of his freshman year of college. He lived at home and commuted to school, working part-time evenings and weekends. His difficulties began when he was laid off from his job as a sales clerk. He soon found another job as a bus

boy but resigned after about one month, feeling that the job was tedious and demeaning. After this he spent time alone at home evenings and weekends, watching television and sleeping longer hours. He reports that about this time his mood changed and he became mildly depressed and increasingly anxious. He found that he began to have difficulty with concentration on his studies.

Over the next several months he noticed a variety of disturbing changes. He began to feel that radio and TV shows had stories and observations that seemed to focus on his problems. He became suspicious of schoolmates and teachers, and it sometimes seemed to him that their faces changed shape, becoming distorted in ways that were hostile and menacing.

He had always been shy with women and had dated very little. He had always had some worries about his sexual identity, but these now increased greatly in intensity. He began to be preoccupied with fears that he was homosexual. He began to feel that others suspected he was homosexual and he watched carefully for any subtle indication that schoolmates or acquaintances questioned his sexual identity. As his symptoms worsened he began to have fleeting suicidal ideation.

Despite his problems with concentration he continued to attend freshman college classes and, although his grades deteriorated, he managed to finish his freshman year. Once summer vacation began his condition worsened rapidly. He became more severely depressed, with guilty ruminations, loss of appetite, and sleep disturbance. He gradually became delusional, disorganized, and intensely suicidal. In the month prior to his admission he was sleeping 12 to 14 hours per day and had experienced a 20 pound weight loss.

Scott's prodromal experience is rich with opportunities for useful psychotherapeutic exploration. The very gradual development of a wide variety of prodromal symptoms makes it possible to explore the complexities of the prodromal experience in detail and help Scott to learn to recognize the early development of prepsychotic symptoms. Social withdrawal, depression, difficulty in concentration, sleep disturbance, loss of appetite, visual illusions, sexual preoccupations, and suicidal ideation can all be identified, explored, and used as guidelines for resuming treatment with antipsychotic medication in the future. Even if Scott has difficulty recognizing some of these prodromal symptoms, the richness and variety of his prodro-

mal experience makes it likely that at least one or two prodromal symptoms can be utilized as signals for the resumption of
antipsychotic medication.

In contrast, Gary's history is one which presents a formida-
ble set of difficulties for therapist and patient in identifying and
aborting a recurrent psychotic episode.

Gary is a 22-year-old single college senior. He was hospitalized
for a first psychotic episode shortly after he returned to college
from home after the Easter holiday. He had done reasonably well
during his first three years of college. He worked hard and had a
B average, although his grades deteriorated in the first semester
of his senior year. He had an active social life on campus although
he occasionally had difficulty getting along with his roommates.
For several years he had been a heavy user of marijuana and also
drank heavily on weekends. During his junior year he regularly
used PCP, LSD, and cocaine. He used amphetamines regularly
for both recreational purposes and to help him with his studying.

During the Christmas vacation at the end of the first semester
of his senior year he reported being depressed. He was withdrawn and less active than usual, sleeping a good deal of the
time. He was concerned about his recent poor school performance
and was determined to do better during the coming semester. He
returned to school and redoubled his efforts at studying. His marijuana use and amphetamine use increased at the same time. He
used amphetamines frequently to help him study late at night and
also for recreation—he lead an unusually frenetic social life and
got very little sleep.

When he went home for the Easter holiday he continued to be
unusually active. He looked and felt tense and driven. He talked
rapidly and was irritable and guarded when friends and family
expressed concern. While at a party with friends he suddenly became fearful that someone had put hallucinogenic drugs in his
drink. He became so frightened that he ran out of the party and
his family later found him wandering on the highway. He returned home and took a sleeping pill which helped him to sleep a
good part of the next 24 hours. When he awoke he seemed "back
to normal." Three days later he returned to school.

The day after he arrived at school he again became agitated
and fearful that he had been drugged. He soon began to insist
that someone wanted to kill him and he became agitated and disorganized. Over the next several hours he became so disturbed

that he had to be subdued by police and brought to an emergency room in restraints.

In exploring his prodromal experience Gary was able to identify comparatively little that might be of value in alerting him to a recurrent psychotic episode. He tended to believe that drugs were solely responsible for his psychotic illness. In addition, he felt that once he became suspicious of other people he was so caught up in his suspicions that it was unlikely that he could recognize his fears as a symptom of impending psychosis.

He was able to identify the sense of feeling under great pressure as one important element in the prodromal experience. In addition, his increased anxiety and sleeplessness could also be explored as useful warning signs, although Gary tended to insist that both of these symptoms were the result of his increased use of amphetamines. However, he eventually came to understand that increased anxiety and sleeplessness could be regarded as prodromal symptoms of recurrent psychosis even if they were caused by drug use.

Gary could understand that the drug use itself was the central precipitant in his psychotic illness. As such, drug use could be regarded with some accuracy as the warning sign most useful for him. He made it clear that he understood this concept, although he confessed that he enjoyed using drugs too much to relinquish them entirely. He was convinced that a more moderate use of recreational drugs would be reasonably safe, particularly if he avoided using amphetamines when under pressure.

Once he made it clear that he regarded *any* recreational drug use as unacceptably dangerous, Gary's therapist had little choice but to tolerate Gary's wish to continue "more moderate" use of drugs. Any attempt to forbid him to use drugs would only exclude discussion of drug use from the treatment and make it impossible for the therapist to know when he was at maximum risk. Since drug use is most likely the single most important prodromal symptom of recurrent psychosis for this patient it is important that Gary be able to tell his therapist about which drugs he is using and how often he is using them.

Hypomania as a Prodromal Symptom

Hypomania is a particularly important prodromal symptom for patients with bipolar disorders. Unfortunately, it is especially difficult for patients to identify hypomania as a warning sign of impending psychosis. The ''improvement'' they experience when hypomanic seems quite genuine to them and the therapist may also be deceived into thinking that their joint therapeutic efforts are finally bearing fruit. The clinician should keep in mind that lasting improvements come slowly and only after considerable effort. Dramatic improvement is suspect and is more than likely to be a signal that decompensation is imminent. It is usually an ominous sign when an individual *suddenly* regains lost confidence, approaches the world with unexpected energy and enthusiasm, or experiences a ''breakthrough'' which promises to make it possible to quickly master all difficulties, as the following case illustrates.

Pamela, a single 22-year-old, has a long history of erratic behavior and mood swings. These difficulties began early in adolescence and gradually worsened during her last two years in high school. Despite these problems, she was able to complete her high school studies and she was accepted at a competitive college.

She found it difficult to be away from her family and she suffered periods of homesickness so severe that she began to miss classes and had difficulty concentrating. After several months she became quite irritable, frequently picking fights with close acquaintances or roommates. Eventually she was asked to withdraw from school. Her advisor suggested that her poor academic performance stemmed directly from her emotional problems and he recommended that she seek psychotherapeutic help.

Pamela returned home and spent most of her time alone watching TV. Sleep and appetite both increased. After several weeks her parents became alarmed at her withdrawn behavior and insisted that she begin psychotherapy and look for a job. She reluctantly began outpatient treatment and, after several false starts, took a job at a nearby factory.

After about two months her mood improved. She began to feel more optimistic and she became less withdrawn. She approached both her work and her treatment with growing enthusiasm, and her parents and therapist were delighted with the change. However, after several weeks she became energized and euphoric. Her sleep and appetite now decreased, and she began to lose weight. She was soon fired from her job because she began talking incessantly about the need for major changes in the design and organization of the factory. She insisted that she was dismissed because the foreman knew that she was about to get his job.

Her parents and therapist conferred and agreed that Pamela required hospital treatment. Pamela resisted hospitalization strenuously, moving rapidly from the home of one friend to another in order to avoid her parents. During the two weeks before her admission her symptoms worsened steadily. She became pressured, excitable, and grandiose. As she became frankly psychotic she wrote volumes of incoherent poetry, was indiscriminately sexually active, and provoked a fight with a stranger on the street. She did not sleep at all during the three days prior to admission.

Patients can learn to recognize depressive symptoms as part of a prepsychotic prodrome, or at least as signs that their moods are not properly under control. However, hypomanic patients are particularly prone to lose whatever insight they have acquired into their prodromal symptoms as their judgment is swept away on tide of unshakeable confidence. Euphoria commonly causes distortions in memory and judgment which can quickly nullify months of painstaking exploratory work. Perhaps more than any other, the symptom of hypomania requires that the patient be thoroughly prepared in advance if there is to be any prospect of intervening successfully and aborting an impending decompensation.

A careful and detailed reconstruction of the patient's earlier hypomanic symptoms can make it possible for the therapist to prepare the patient to recognize their recurrence. The patient can use this reconstruction to understand that he is likely to feel so good during the hypomanic period that he will find it extremely difficult to believe that there is any danger. Consequently, the patient is likely to dispute his therapist's observation that he is in danger of relapse. If he is forewarned that this is likely to be the case, he may be prepared to accept his clinician's judgment despite an intuitive conviction that he is better than ever.

Still, despite these preparations, the therapist's attempt to alert the patient to hypomanic prodromal symptoms may produce only an argument which quickly leads to a therapeutic stalemate. At that point the therapist can only remind the patient that this was precisely the sort of difficulty that they tried to anticipate and avoid. Even if the patient ignores the therapist and goes on to decompensation, he may be able to use the second experience of decompensation to learn to recognize hypomania when it occurs, or at least to pay attention to warnings from others. Often manic patients must decompensate a second or third time before they can learn to deal with prodromal symptoms effectively or acknowledge that continuous prophylaxis is necessary.

Some patients, particularly those with a history of many psychotic episodes and compromised function, derive so much satisfaction from their euphoria and grandiosity that they are reluctant to give it up. Such patients have little motivation to learn to control psychotic symptoms and they are unlikely to do so unless their deterioration can be reversed by some structured rehabilitation program.

When Prodromal Symptoms Occur

For those patients who develop prodromal symptoms following decrease or discontinuation of medication, treatment with antipsychotic medication should be prompt and vigorous. Given the length of time it takes for antipsychotic medication to be effective, early treatment with full antipsychotic doses of medication is usually essential. The patient should be prepared for the high doses of medication which may be employed. This forewarning is particularly important since an unprepared patient may be terrified by a proposed dramatic increase in the dose of medication. If he does not expect and understand that prodromal symptoms often must be treated with comparatively high doses of medication, the patient is likely to conclude that the clinician is greatly alarmed at his condition and is reacting so vigorously because the situation is desperate. The panic which this can trigger in the patient can cause prodromal symptoms to spiral out of control long before the medication can have any useful effect. Thus, as soon as the dose of medication is lowered for the first time, the patient should be made to understand that if prodromal symptoms appear, it probably will be necessary to raise the dose well above its maintenance level to maximize its effect. Antiparkinson agents may be necessary also and the patient should be forewarned of this as well. Most patients are frightened and disheartened at the appearance of prodromal symptoms, but a properly prepared patient may be able to accept the clinician's reassurance that the intervention is early enough to prevent relapse and that the high doses of medication do not mean matters are out of control.

Learning from Relapse

Inevitably there will be errors and missed opportunities and some patients will relapse despite the best efforts of both clinician and patient. Despite the distress and disruption involved, each relapse offers the opportunity, during the subsequent convalescent period, for the patient and therapist to review together the events leading up to the psychotic episode, including the prodromal symptoms. New symptoms may have been observed that can be more reliable indicators of impending relapse. Prodromal symptoms which were missed by either the patient or the therapist can be reviewed in detail and the observational skills of both can be sharpened. A patient who was unable to recognize prodromal symptoms even when they were called to his attention can now examine that process to learn to react more constructively in the future. Patients who harbor doubts about whether they are actually vulnerable to relapse can now be more nearly certain that it is necessary to invest time and energy in reducing their vulnerability to recurrent psychosis. Thus, the clinician should bear in mind that, when relapse occurs in the context of a strong psychotherapeutic relationship, the patient may be able to learn a great deal from the experience, so much so that the relapse can become a positive turning point in the treatment. At times the opportunity to work intensively with a trusted therapist during one or more relapses can make possible a fundamental change in the patient's grasp of his illness, improve medication compliance, and spur the patient's interest in psychotherapeutic work.

There are, of course, some patients who are either unable or unwilling to learn even from repeated decompensations. If, after multiple episodes, the patient is unable to make any progress in this regard, chronic maintenance treatment with prophylactic medication may be the only workable alternative. Another possibility may be a treatment contract in which some responsible family member, employer, or friend learns to observe the patient for prodromal symptoms and agrees to contact the clinician should they appear. If the patient can be induced to accept this arrangement, it may be possible to use intermittent treatment with medication despite the patient's inability to recognize prodromal symptoms.

Patients Who Manage Their Own Medications

Once patients have demonstrated that they are capable of recognizing prodromal symptoms and of starting medication in time to abort a relapse, they may be taught to manage their own medication. This management should be done first under the supervision of the clinician to be certain that the patient medicates himself with the appropriate doses and for suitable periods of time. Ultimately, such patients may be able to monitor their clinical state and to regulate medication entirely on their own, seeing the clinician as infrequently as every two or three months. Because of the risk of tardive dyskinesia, patients must be seen periodically even if they can regulate their medication entirely independently. An example follows.

A 36-year-old, single woman has been followed in treatment for 10 years following her first psychiatric hospitalization for psychotic symptoms. After a year of intermittent psychotic symptoms she had become catatonic and was finally hospitalized. After two turmoil-filled years of intensive outpatient treatment, during which time she refused medication and was again hospitalized, she was able to begin consistent work in psychotherapy and her medication compliance was excellent. After two additional years of less intensive treatment she was self-supporting and free of psychotic symptoms, although she remained an eccentric and relatively isolated person. By the end of the fourth year of treatment she had learned to regulate her own antipsychotic medication and could intelligently decide when to take the comparatively high levels of antipsychotic medication her condition occasionally required. Since that time she has been seen at monthly intervals to renew her medication and to discuss problems and changes in her life.

Psychotherapeutic Management of Tardive Dyskinesia

The appearance of symptoms of tardive dyskinesia inaugurates a dismaying and potentially catastrophic development in the treatment of patients with psychotic disorders. The clinician often must bring considerable skill and effort to bear on the problem to avert a major disruption of the treatment. Not only is the patient almost invariably upset and frightened, but the fact that neuroleptic medications are usually promptly discontinued decreases the patient's protection against relapse at a particularly stressful time.

Disciplined clinical management of this distressing development depends heavily on early detection of the disorder and adequate preparation of both patient and therapist. Early detection of minimal symptoms of tardive dyskinesia reduces the likelihood that the patient will respond with a panicky urgency, making thoughtful planning impossible. Any clinician working with patients taking neuroleptic medication must have thorough training in the early detection of symptoms of tardive dyskinesia. Merely reading about the disorder is not adequate training. Clinicians need the opportunity to observe patients with early symptoms (either directly or in motion pictures). The clinician should be ready to propose an orderly strategy for coping with the crisis. A frightened and obviously uncertain clinician is likely to lose both the confidence of his patient and control of the treatment. The first step may involve referring the patient to an experienced colleague to confirm the diagnosis.

The possibility of tardive dyskinesia should always be discussed with patients when informed consent is obtained, usually early in the convalescent phase of treatment. Once the disorder is detected a detailed review of the syndrome with the patient and with appropriate family members is essential as a prelude to the presentation of treatment options. In presenting these options, it is important that the clinician make clear his recommendations and the reasoning behind them. Treatment strategies may vary greatly, depending on the severity of the patient's condition and his stage in treatment. For example, if the patient is in the early convalescent phase of recovery, the clinician may recommend that he continue on low dose neuroleptic medication. Other patients may be in the process of discontinuing medication when symptoms are detected and an acceleration of that process may be the next appropriate step. However, for many patients the rapid discontinuation of medication following the diagnosis of tardive dyskinesia is an untimely and serious disruption of an orderly treatment plan, and the situation can be further complicated by the fact that the dyskinesia often worsens once medication is stopped.

When the medication is discontinued, the clinician should expect to work intensively with the patient (and possibly with family members) on a strategy to adopt when and if prodromal symptoms appear. Many of the patient's reservations about medication are likely to resurface under this kind of stress, and the therapeutic alliance is often severely strained. Denial of symptoms or of vulnerability to relapse are common. In addition, some patients are aware of the risks, but are so troubled by the prospect of a disfiguring and irreversible movement disorder that they refuse medication anyway.

In cases where the treatment was going well and the patient is nearly ready to discontinue medication, the appearance of symptoms of tardive dyskinesia may be managed with only relatively limited disruption of treatment. However, when the patient is ill-prepared to discontinue medication, the disruption of treatment is properly regarded as a major crisis, and the clinician should be ready to respond accordingly. Family involvement in decision making and monitoring of the patient's clinical state is usually necessary. Should the patient show early signs of decompensation, the preliminary work done with the patient and family may make it possible to work collaboratively to avert a full psychotic decompensation. This situation puts the patient in a frightening dilemma—he must choose between psychosis and tardive dyskinesia. In this desperate situation the patient and family are likely to rely heavily on the therapists's advice and guidance. The clinician may need to spend considerable time explaining treatment options and offering advice about which alternatives are likely to be least damaging.

Psychotherapy After Convalescence

In many cases the psychotherapeutic work of the convalescent period extends well beyond the time when the patient has returned to premorbid levels of function. A jointly agreed upon strategy for the control of long-term vulnerability to relapse is sometimes achieved only after years of work and effort. However, for many patients the period after convalescence is a turning point in the treatment. It is during this time that patient and therapist may gradually decide either to move toward termination of treatment or toward additional psychotherapeutic work on preexisting problems in the patient's personality and function. The therapeutic effort expended throughout the acute and convalescent phases is designed not only to prevent psychotic illness from dominating the whole of the patient's future, but also to prepare him for the opportunity to use psychotherapy for growth and progress.

Some patients do not take advantage of this opportunity. They may view the psychosis as the only significant problem requiring professional attention and may see little or no role for psychotherapy once vulnerability to relapse is adequately controlled. These patients are likely to regard treatment as essentially complete once premorbid function is restored and the threat of relapse appears to be under control. Having achieved these goals, they may decrease the frequency of contacts with the clinician, and use their subsequent sessions to have their condition monitored periodically. These patients are often the sort who view their disorder as a kind of "chemical imbalance" which has been corrected by the medication. For example, some patients taking lithium describe their illness as a "salt deficiency," and they conceive of treatment as the correction of this "deficiency" through the use of "lithium salts." Some patients even cite "evidence" for this view by reporting that "blood tests have shown that I have a low level of lithium."

A number of clinicians apparently regard this view of psychosis as a "chemical imbalance" as an essentially accurate conception of psychotic disorders. Most clinicians are aware that this idea is a gross oversimplification at best, but may be tempted to teach patients to think of their illness in this way, hoping that it will increase the likelihood of their compliance with a medication regimen, especially in the early phases of treatment. Unfortunately, these concepts frequently cause difficulty in later phases of treatment when patients fail to take advantage of the opportunity for psychotherapeutic work on problems which medication cannot correct.

Beginning Exploratory Treatment

For the first year or so after the acute psychotic episode, treatment is largely concerned with the problems of stabilizing the patient and fostering recovery. Restoring premorbid function and protecting the patient against relapse are tasks which largely preclude extensive exploration of deficiencies in personality and development. Thus, for most patients the first opportunity to do any sustained exploratory work comes during the latter portion of the convalescent period when exploration of prodromal symptoms of psychosis is an important part of developing a strategy to deal with long-term vulnerability to relapse. This work gives the patient an opportunity to experience exploratory treatment in a modified form, while giving the therapist an opportunity to observe the patient's level of motivation and capacity for introspection.

Only a minority of patients are able to make substantial use of additional exploratory treatment. While developing a strategy for long-term protection against relapse, this minority may begin to identify other problems which require attention. As this work proceeds, the patient and therapist can jointly define some of these problems as possible subjects for additional psychotherapeutic effort.

Some patients cannot or will not identify any problems requiring additional psychotherapeutic work, although in many instances the patient's deficits may be obvious to the clinician. Other patients may be aware of problems but may need time for further consolidation of their recovery from psychosis before embarking on additional psychotherapeutic work. For these patients the need to stay alert to the possibility of relapse may be as much as they can cope with in the period immediately after convalescence. They may need several years before they are able to return and reenter treatment which focuses on an exploration of prexisting problems.

Patients who do not require a period of consolidation at the end of convalescence may be able to shift directly into an exploratory phase of treatment and some even increase the frequency of sessions of this juncture. For a minority of these patients it is possible to discontinue medication altogether and move toward a typical, dynamically-oriented, exploratory treatment.

Sam, a 25-year-old graduate student, was hospitalized for a psychotic episode precipitated by the break up of a long-standing relationship with his girlfriend. After living together for several years, the girlfriend developed a central nervous system illness which left her physically crippled and mentally impaired. Although he expended considerable effort in caring for her, the patient felt burdened by these obligations and trapped in the relationship. After considerable agonizing he finally moved out of their apartment and several months later suffered a psychotic decompensation.

The patient worked hard in therapy and his medication compliance was excellent. After one year in treatment medication was gradually discontinued and the patient began an active exploration of the events leading to the psychotic experience. In addition, he became intrigued with the content of the psychotic experience and the developmental issues surrounding it. He was able to make use of the psychotherapeutic work to gain perspective on the acute illness and in addition he was able to address some long-standing difficulties he had in his close relationships.

This highly motivated patient was able to take the initiative in conducting his therapy and he permitted the therapist to take a neutral exploratory stance. As the therapy progressed, the patient was able to return to school and he later formed a more satisfying relationship with a different woman.

Most patients approach exploratory treatment burdened by a variety of handicaps such as limited intelligence, high levels of vulnerability to relapse, limited capacity for introspection, severe residual symptoms, and cognitive deficits. These patients require a modified treatment which combines exploratory work with a supportive and structured style. The pace of this modified treatment is usually quite slow. Clinician and patient may find the slow progress frustrating and both must resist the temptation to resort to impulsive attempts to increase the pace. Anxiety and emotional arousal are likely to evoke fears of relapse in these patients, requiring additional reassurance and exploratory effort and slowing the pace of treatment. Progress is usually made through a long series of small steps with frequent ups and downs. The therapist should be prepared for much hesitation and uncertainty from the patient and, at moments of particular difficulty, the clinician may need to be active, encouraging, and directive. On the other hand, there may be periods of comparatively sustained exploratory work.

Beverly, a single 28-year-old, had a history of two psychotic episodes. In the five years since her last episode she made steady progress. Her neuroleptic medication was discontinued after two years and she has been maintained since on lithium alone. Her second psychotic episode was precipitated by the breakup of her first serious romantic involvement. She had grown deeply attached to a man who wanted only a casual relationship. When he broke off the affair, she found the experience unbearably painful. In the months following the breakup her medication compliance was poor and she eventually required hospitalization for a recurrence of psychotic symptoms.

During her convalescence from this psychotic episode she returned to work but avoided relationships with men altogether. Some months after her neuroleptic medication was discontinued she was less frightened of relapse and began occasional tentative sexual involvements. Her first experiences were casual encounters with men she met at bars and she deliberately avoided any emotional involvement with them. She was pleased that she was still able to attract men, but found these "one night stands" left her feeling used and degraded.

While applauding her courage in risking relations with men once again, the clinician observed that the benefits of these encounters were undermined by their destructive effect on her self-esteem. On several occasions the therapist told her "I think it is safe for you to try to do better."

Exploration of her fears that rejection might precipitate a relapse helped to improve her confidence to the point where she could risk more sustained involvements with men who were interested in more than a sexual experience. Over the next year she embarked on two successive relationships which, while more satisfying, involved men who were not available for a permanent commitment. Much of the psychotherapeutic work during this period focused on Beverly's difficulties in trusting men and her fears of intimacy which derived from her parent's unhappy and turbulent marriage. Only after nearly five years had elapsed since the psychotic episode was she able to risk involvement with a more eligible man.

Emotional Stresses for the Therapist

Psychotherapeutic work with psychotic patients can be demanding, anxiety-provoking, and turbulent for the therapist.

Problems for the clinician during the supportive and didactic work of the convalescent phase are likely to be because the work is frequently tedious, frustrating, and repetitious. The disagreements and tensions between the patient and therapist during convalescence are generally low-key and static, while progress is slow at best. Overall, however, intensive psychotherapeutic work with psychotic patients can provoke disturbing reactions in the clinician. The inner world of the psychotic patient is often disconcerting and threatening, and coping with the unfolding of this inner world requires high levels of skill, concentration, and stamina for the therapist. During the course of intensive exploratory work a psychotic patient can evoke intense frustration, loathing, attraction, rage, anxiety, and disorganization in the therapist, even when the therapy is progressing well. The clinical management of psychotic transference no longer seems to get the attention in training programs it had several decades ago. It is perhaps worth reemphasizing that psychosis, after all, is frightening to observe and that the clinician's experience of an episodic, painful fear of disorganization, attack, and loss of control is probably a normal and predictable consequence of intense involvement with psychotic patients.

Because exploratory work with psychotic patients is so stressful, clinicians should periodically review their caseloads to insure that they have patients who present a reasonable variety of diagnostic and therapeutic problems with an appropriate range of severity of pathology. When a clinician finds his work unusually distressing, an unbalanced and emotionally overwhelming caseload should be considered as the most likely immediate source of the difficulty. Clinicians also should take care in the scheduling of their patients. Especially difficult or demanding patients should not be scheduled consecutively. It may be useful for the clinician to review each day's schedule in advance to see if there are particular hours he dreads. If there are several such hours in succession, a change in the scheduling may be advisable. Clinicians who choose to do intensive exploratory work with severely disturbed patients should probably continue to have supervision for several years after they complete their training. The availability of experienced supervisors can make the first several years of independent practice far less painful and anxiety-provoking.

Experienced clinicians also can profit greatly by having ready access to colleagues with whom they can discuss distressing cases, thus relieving their anxiety. Even senior clinicians may find that regular case discussions with colleagues help maintain perspective and prevent private therapeutic style from becoming excessively idiosyncratic in response to patient-generated emotional stress. In this context the clinician may be able to examine the content of emotionally stressful reactions to patients to understand and resolve as far as possible the issues generating the distress. Finally, the clinician must have the capacity to refuse a referral that would add too much stress to an already draining caseload, even though he has therapeutic time available and needs the work. A sensitivity to personal vulnerabilities and limitations is something every therapist should cultivate.

Tension Between Medication and Exploratory Treatment

To some extent antipsychotic medication and exploratory psychotherapy are inherently at cross purposes, and there is inevitably some tension generated by their combined use in treatment. Medication implies the risk of relapse. It suggests that stability is paramount and that any emotional distress should be examined to determine if it represents a prepsychotic symptom. Exploratory psychotherapy suggests the possibility of progress beyond the status quo. It implies that the emotional distress generated by exploratory effort is a necessary concomitant of developmental progress and is an inevitable part of a successful treatment.

This tension between antipsychotic medication and exploratory psychotherapy is nowhere more evident then when a patient in a post-convalescent phase of treatment reports symptoms that have been previously identified as possible prodromal symptoms of recurrent psychosis. In some cases it is clear that the patient is suffering early signs of psychotic decompensation. However, often the significance of the patient's symptoms is ambiguous and both patient and clinician are faced with an urgent problem in differential diagnosis. Together they must determine quickly if the symptoms represent impending relapse or if they are manifestations of anxiety generated by the stress of psychotherapeutic work, or both.

If the patient is suffering from prepsychotic symptoms, prompt treatment with full antipsychotic doses of medication offers the best chance of aborting or controlling a possible relapse. Exploratory psychotherapy is stressful and, at times, can precipitate relapse in vulnerable patients. However, these symptoms may represent either appropriate anxiety and arousal in response to psychotherapeutic progress or they may be manifestations of unconscious resistance to exploratory effort and may not be early signs of relapse. For example, in reporting symptoms the patient may be unconsciously testing the therapist to see if he is confident that the therapeutic process is safe. In other instances the patient may be alarmed at the emergence of emotionally charged material in the course of exploratory treatment and may exaggerate symptoms in an unconscious effort to deflect the treatment into a focus on the risk of relapse. In these instances medication is contraindicated and the reported symptoms are best explored as resistance. Treating these symptoms with antipsychotic medication is likely to intensify the patient's fears and to disrupt the psychotherapeutic work.

Distinguishing between genuine prodromal symptoms, appropriate distress, and "resistance symptoms" is sometimes quite difficult. The matter is further complicated by the fact that some patients who have mild chronic residual psychotic symptoms may occasionally have periods when psychotic symptoms increase briefly in the course of psychotherapeutic work. These mild intensifications of chronic symptoms do not necessarily require treatment with additional antipsychotic medication. For example a patient's quiescent, chronic delusional concerns may increase in intensity when exploratory treatment becomes stressful. Similarly, some chronically psychotic patients while in remission may have an increase in paranoid symptoms or brief periods of increased confusion or depression which are a direct result of exploratory treatment and which do not necessarily herald relapse.

The distinction is best made by carefully exploring the symptoms with the patient and assessing whether the exploration leads to resolution or intensification of symptoms. In general, genuine prodromal symptoms intensify and "resistance symptoms" tend to resolve rapidly with exploration and reassurance. However, it is essential that the clinician make the assessment promptly, since a prodromal period may last only a short time before the development of florid psychotic symptoms.

Beverly, the patient described earlier this chapter, has a history of two psychotic episodes, but has been successfully maintained on lithium. During her post-convalescent treatment, psychotherapeutic work focused on her fear of intimacy with men. Because her second psychotic episode was precipitated by the break-up of a romantic relationship, she was understandably anxious when, for the first time since her psychotic illness, she began a sustained relationship with a man.

After an argument with her boyfriend, she returned home and experienced an increase in symptoms of anxiety and depression. Over the next several hours her symptoms worsened and she eventually placed an emergency call to her therapist, complaining that she was experiencing "periods of confusion and hallucinations." When she met her clinician the next morning she suggested immediate resumption of full antipsychotic doses of medication.

The therapist carefully explored with her the events of the last several days and asked her to describe her symptoms in detail. In the process he noted that she was able to stay in good contact and

to recount the details of her symptoms in a reasonably well-orga-
nized way. When asked to describe her hallucinations she reported that while alone at home the previous evening she became
severely anxious and fearful of relapse. As her anxiety worsened
she thought she heard voices calling her name.

She was able to acknowledge that the argument with her boyfriend had frightened her and stirred up memories of her earlier
psychotic episode. She said she was convinced that her symptoms were a warning that she was attempting too much in her
treatment. The therapist made it clear that he disagreed. While explaining that her distress was understandable, he told her that, in
his opinion, she did not appear to be in the early stages of relapse.
No additional medication was prescribed. However, a brief meeting was scheduled for the following morning as a precaution. At
that time the patient's symptoms had vanished and she was
much relieved.

When the therapist is not a physician, ideal management of
an assessment of this sort should involve both clinicians. This
is most easily done if the patient can meet with both clinicians
immediately. Since a joint meeting is often impossible to arrange at short notice, the assessment should be conducted by
the primary clinician and consultation with the psychiatrist
should take place before arriving at a final decision. Because of
scheduling problems, it may sometimes be necessary for the
psychiatrist to prescribe medication after a telephone conversation with the primary clinician. When this occurs the psychiatrist should attempt to see the patient in person as soon as possible.

Since assessments of this sort are difficult and usually hur-
ried, miscalculations and errors are inevitable. Because the
stakes are high it is important that the clinician take care not to
let anxiety prompt an impulsive act. In ambiguous cases a delay of 24 hours is usually enough to clarify matters. The risk involved here is justified by the greater diagnostic accuracy that it
permits. The therapist should also take care that his wishes and
biases do not distort his judgment. Clinicians who are insecure
about the stresses and turmoil of exploratory work may be unconsciously relieved to return to the more familiar territory of

medication and vulnerability to relapse. Alternatively, a therapist may be so invested in his patient's successful progress in treatment that he is reluctant to identify an ominous prodromal symptom.

In some instances the clinical picture is so ambiguous and confusing that it is impossible to draw a clear distinction between prodromal symptoms and "resistance symptoms." Where the therapist knows the patient well and feels he has a good grasp of the patient's typical pattern of symptoms, he may elect to accept the risks involved and continue to treat the patient without starting prophylactic medication. However, in most cases, faced with such a difficult situation the most prudent course for the clinician is to assume that relapse is likely and to respond accordingly, giving the patient appropriate doses of antipsychotic medication to abort a possible decompensation.

Having done so, the clinician may find the patient badly frightened and discouraged. Under such circumstances the patient may conclude that exploratory effort in therapy is unacceptably risky and is to be avoided. The clinician may need to expend considerable time and effort in reassuring the patient that exploratory treatment may still be a workable possibility. In some instances, possible increased vulnerability to relapse during stressful periods of treatment can be controlled effectively by having the patient take antipsychotic medication in anticipation of the increased stress. Unlike the strategy in which antipsychotic medication is used intermittently whenever the patient experiences prodromal symptoms, this strategy employs intermittent medication whenever the patient is attempting a new and particularly stressful change in life or treatment, but before the appearance of any troublesome or ambiguous symptoms.

> Roland, a 21-year-old, suffered his first psychotic episode at the age of 18 while a freshman undergraduate at college. After a hospital stay of six weeks he withdrew from school and returned to his parents' home. He found work as a laboratory technician and began intensive outpatient treatment. He took his therapy seri-

ously and was a conscientious and compliant patient. Over the next 14 months his antipsychotic medication was gradually decreased and finally discontinued. However, on two occasions when he attempted to leave his parents' home for his own apartment or to return to school as a fulltime student, he was unable to make the change because of the appearance of frightening symptoms. Whenever preparations for these proposed changes reached an advanced stage, Roland suffered increasingly severe symptoms of anxiety, restlessness, sleeplessness, and difficulty in concentration.

In the course of his work in psychotherapy, Roland had gained some understanding that the combined stresses of leaving home, making new friends, and dealing with more intense academic competition had played an important role in precipitating his illness. In addition, he had conducted a careful review of his earlier prodromal symptoms and was very much aware that the symptoms he suffered in preparing for these new changes were reminiscent of the earlier prodromal symptoms. Since, in both instances, neither Roland nor his therapist could be certain that these symptoms were not early signs of relapse, a course of prophylactic antipsychotic medication was begun. The resulting distress prompted Roland to change his plans in both instances and to avoid major changes in his life situation.

After considerable discussion, Roland and his clinician agreed that a course of prophylactic treatment with antipsychotic medication would be helpful in anticipation of these stressful changes. Both agreed that it was not at all clear that the medication was necessary to prevent relapse, but both felt that the uncertainty added too much anxiety to an already difficult task. Accordingly, Roland started on medication two months before returning to school as a fulltime student. He continued on the medication through the first semester of school and gradually discontinued it midway through the second semester after his return.

In some patients this anticipatory use of medication may be the most effective prophylactic strategy. Highly compliant patients, who are clearly vulnerable to stress and who become especially anxious and frightened by the idea of waiting until prodromal symptoms appear, may be better able to use this sort of approach. Similarly, bipolar patients with cyclic patterns of recurrent psychosis are best treated with this anticipatory strategy.

Exploring the Psychotic Experience

Patients may express interest in exploring the content of the psychotic experience and they may solicit the therapist's assistance in understanding unconscious meanings of a variety of symptoms suffered during the psychotic episode. Other patients express little or no interest in the content of their psychosis and actively avoid attempts to explore this material should the therapist suggest they do so. As the exploratory phase of treatment unfolds, it usually becomes clear which patients can make use of this kind of exploration, although usually even those patients who are highly motivated to explore the psychotic content are able to do so only tentatively and intermittently.

Successful exploratory treatment does not in any way require exploration of the content of the psychotic experience, and the clinician should bear this in mind when dealing with the matter with a resistant patient. The major issues important to a successful exploratory therapy can emerge in a variety of ways and exploration of the psychotic content is only one possibility—not necessarily the most useful or productive. The same basic material may emerge in the patient's dreams or fantasies in a way which causes less anxiety and resistance. As the patient struggles to master obstacles to improved function, the underlying conflicts involved may emerge in their clearest and most accessible form as the treatment focuses directly on these difficulties.

For those patients who are able to make direct use of the content of the psychotic experience in their exploratory work, the process usually evolves in several stages. These patients typically begin by undertaking a detailed review of the psychotic experience early in the exploratory phase of treatment. This is often a natural outgrowth of the earlier exploration of the prodromal experience which was undertaken toward the end of the convalescent period. It is usually an attempt to reconstruct and organize recollections of the psychotic experience, an effort which often generates a broad range of emotions ranging from embarrassment, revulsion, dismay, and horror to

amusement, pride, nostalgia, and pleasure. In assisting the patient at this stage the clinician functions best as a receptive lis-
tener who helps keep the material in perspective, corrects gross
factual errors, and helps the patient begin to deal with the
sense of alienation and stigma these details evoke. The process
of reviewing psychotic experience can make it possible for the
patient to reduce the intensely charged and disturbing quality
of this material and make it more readily accessible later in
treatment. The patient's early speculations about the significance of the psychotic content should be noted by the clinician,
who should make it clear that he will reserve judgment about
these meanings until there is an opportunity to explore the material in greater detail.

In some instances patients return to this material seldom, if
at all, as later exploratory work progresses. Other patients return regularly for more elaborate exploration as related issues
emerge in ongoing treatment. The clinician can test the patient's capacity to make use of this material by raising relevant
details of the psychotic content at appropriate moments in exploratory work, awaiting the patient's reaction and observing
his ability to make use of the material as treatment unfolds.

Vacations

When treating psychotic patients clinicians should plan vacations with particular care. This is especially true early in treatment when the therapeutic alliance may be tenuous and the patient's vulnerability to relapse is high. When the patient is in
the acute phase of illness or during the period immediately after discharge from a hospital, vacations are so difficult to manage successfully that it is probably best if the therapist avoids
accepting new patients when a vacation is imminent.

The patient should be informed of the time and duration of
the clinician's absence well in advance, and plans for back up
coverage should be explained in detail and on several occasions. If the clinician is going to be absent for a day or two, the

patient's sessions should be rescheduled if at all possible. Even if the patient is not scheduled for a session during the therapist's brief absence (for example over a weekend), it is still advisable to tell the patient that the therapist will not be available and that another clinician will be providing coverage. Patients in the acute and convalescent phases of illness need a clear sense that they are being taken care of and they are likely to be alarmed if the therapist is suddenly unavailable. (This does not mean that the clinician must be available constantly. However, the patient should feel confident that a telephone call will be returned within a matter of hours.)

When the clinician intends to be on vacation for several weeks or more, it may be important for the patient to meet with the back-up clinician in advance. This gives the patient an opportunity to have someone clearly in mind if contact is needed. In addition, for patients who are particularly fragile or unstable, it may be advisable to schedule regular appointments with the covering clinician. Similarly, patients who are in the process of reducing the dosage of medication at the end of convalescence may need a back-up clinician who has met with them in the recent past and who is aware of what is taking place in the treatment. Failure to do this may lead to the clinician's returning from vacation to find the patient has either decompensated or has resumed full dosages of antipsychotic medication. In general, it is best not to reduce the dose of medication during the month before a vacation so that there is less likelihood of a crisis in treatment during the therapists's absence.

Termination

As treatment progresses most patients are able to assume increasing autonomy both within the treatment and in their personal affairs. Once the convalescent phase of illness is past, patients who are stable are gradually able to exert increasing control over both the content and the intensity of treatment. For the minority of patients who are functioning well and who no longer need antipsychotic medication to prevent relapse, true termination may be possible. More typical are the patients who achieve a measure of control over vulnerability to relapse through continuous or intermittent use of medication and whose psychotherapeutic progress makes it possible for them to function reasonably well in the community. These patients eventually arrive at a functional plateau characterized by varying degrees of residual deficit. Since these patients are often able to manage their own medication and effectively monitor themselves for signs of relapse, their continuing deficits and vulnerability do not require them to continue in intensive psychotherapy. Over a period of time patient and therapist should gradually decide together when intensive psychotherapeutic effort has reached the point of diminishing returns.

This is often a difficult decision, and it should be reached only after considerable discussion and reflection. The therapist can broach the subject tactfully if the therapy appears stagnant, encouraging the patient to join in an assessment of progress and a redefinition of treatment goals. In these discussions the therapist should take care not to impose his views on an undecided patient, but should allow the patient time to sort out his reactions and wishes. In instances where the patient declares himself satisfied with his progress and wishes to end intensive psychotherapeutic work, the therapist can call attention to important remaining problems which might respond to additional therapeutic effort. If the patient does not respond readily to this encouragement, it is probably best to leave well enough alone. Similarly, if a patient insists that he wishes to continue to struggle actively with his problems in order to attain a higher level of function, it is usually best to support these efforts. Since recovering psychotic patients typically progress very slowly in psychotherapy, it often takes many months before it is clear that intensive treatment is no longer productive.

Eventually patients gradually decrease the frequency of therapy sessions. Patients on continuous medication can meet with the clinician every month or two for medication renewal and a review of recent events in the patient's life. Patients who manage their own medication and use it intermittently can initiate contact with the clinician when they deem it necessary. These patients should be instructed to contact the clinician periodically in any case so that they can be checked for tardive dyskinesia.

Some patients resume intensive treatment at intervals when they need help with a particular problem. The therapist should make it clear that this option is always open to patients who have decided to reduce the intensity of treatment.

As the years pass, the relationship between clinician and patient can evolve into a more casual and friendly association in which the clinician is available as a resource and counselor on a continuing, open-ended basis. The ambiguities of termination with these patients are an outgrowth of the typically prolonged course of the disorder, the high incidence and long duration of residual deficits, and the slow pace of psychotherapeutic progress. When patients do well, intensive treatment can easily last four years or more, and treatment relationships lasting ten years and more are not uncommon. Patients often continue to improve and to make use of treatment at many points during these prolonged relationships, though there may be years of limited patient-therapist contact scattered between periods of intensive, productive psychotherapeutic work. Both patients and therapists can be discouraged easily by this prolonged treatment course. A therapist who can be mindful of this lengthy time frame and who can maintain a cautious optimism during the inevitable periods of stagnation is likely to find his efforts slowly but surely rewarded.

Bibliography

BENARROCHE, C.L. and ASTRACHAN, B.M., Interprofessional role relationships in Talbott, J.A. and Caplan, S.R. (eds.), *Psychiatric Administration*, Grune and Stratton, New York, 1982, pp. 223–236.

BOWERS, M.B., JR., *Retreat from Sanity*, Human Sciences Press, New York, 1974.

BROWN, L.J., A short-term hospital program preparing borderline and schizophrenic patients for intensive psychotherapy, *Psychiatry, 44*, 327–336, 1981

CARLSON, G.A. and GOODWIN, F.K., The stages of mania, *Arch. Gen. Psychiatry, 28*, 221–228, 1973.

CARPENTER, W.T. et al., Early intervention vs. continuous pharmacotherapy of schizophrenia, *Psychopharmacology Bulletin, 8*:1, 21–23, 1982.

DOCHERTY, J.P. et al., Psychotherapy and pharmacotherapy: conceptual issues, *Am. J. Psychiatry, 134*, 529–553, 1977.

DOCHERTY, J.P. et al., Stages of onset of schizophrenic psychosis, *Am. J. Psychiatry, 135*:4, 420-426, 1978.

EISENTHAL, S. et al., "Adherence" and the negotiated approach to patienthood, *Arch. Gen. Psychiatry*, 36, 393–398, 1979.

EXTEIN, I. and BOWERS, M.B., JR., State and trait in psychiatric practice, *Am. J. Psychiatry*, *136*, 690–693, 1979.

FARRELL, B.A., The place of psychodynamics in psychiatry, *Brit. J. Psychiatry*, *143*, 1–7, 1983.

FINK, E.B., BRADEN, W., and QUALLS, C.B., Predicting pharmacotherapy outcome by subjective response, *J. Clin. Psychiatry*, *43:7*, 272–275, 1982.

GALDI, J., The causality of depression in schizophrenia, *Brit. J. Psychiatry*, *142*, 621–625, 1983.

GARDOS, G. and COLE, J.O., Maintenance antipsychotic therapy: for whom and how long? Lipton, M.A., DiMascio, A., and Killam, K.F. (eds.), *Psychopharmacology: A Generation of Progress*, Raven Press, New York, 1978, pp. 1169–1178.

GRINSPOON, L., EWALT, JR., and SHADER, R.I., *Schizophrenia: Pharmacotherapy and Psychotherapy*, Robert E. Krieger, Huntington, New York, 1977.

Group for the Advancement of Psychiatry, Report 93: *Pharmacotherapy and Psychotherapy: Paradoxes, Problems, and Progress*, New York GAP, New York, 1975.

GUTHEIL, T.G., Improving patient compliance: psychodynamics in drug prescribing, *Drug Therapy*, *2*, 35–40, 1977.

HAVENS, L.L., Problems with the use of drugs in the psychotherapy of psychotic patients., *Psychiatry*, *26*, 289–296, 1963.

HERZ, M.I. and MELVILLE, C., Relapse in schizophrenia, *Am. J. Psychiatry*, *137:7*, 801–805, 1980.

HERZ, M.I., SZYMANSKI, H.V., and SIMON, J.C., Intermittent medication for stable schizophrenic outpatients: an alternative to maintenance medication, *Am. J. Psychiatry*, *139:7*, 918–922, 1982.

HERZ, M.I., Recognizing and preventing relapse in patients with schizophrenia, *Hospital and Community Psychiatry*, *34: 4*, 344–349, 1984.

HICKS, R. and MCCORMICK, M.G.F., Clinical negotiations in outpatient psychopharmacology in Lazare, A. (ed.), *Outpatient Psychiatry*, Williams and Wilkins, Baltimore, Maryland, 1979, pp. 596–611.

JESTE, D.V. and WYATT, R.J., *Understanding and Treating Tardive Dyskinesia*, Guilford Press, New York, 1982.

KANE, J.M. et al., Low dose neuroleptics in outpatient schizophrenics, *Psychopharmacology Bulletin, 8*:1, 20–21, 1982.

KARASU, T.B., Psychotherapy and pharmacotherapy: toward an integrative model, *Am. J. Psychiatry, 139*:9, 1102–1113, 1982.

LEFF, J. and VAUGHN, C., The interaction of life events and relatives' expressed emotion in schizophrenia and depressive neurosis, *Brit. J. Psychiatry, 136*, 146–153, 1980.

LIDZ, T., FLECK, S., and CORNELISON, A., *Schizophrenia and the Family*, International Universities Press, New York, 1965.

LIEBERMAN, P.B. and STRAUSS, J.S., The recurrence of mania: environmental factors and medical treatment, *Am. J. Psychiatry, 141*:1, 77–79, 1984.

LION, J.R., *The Art of Medicating Psychiatric Patients*, Waverly Press, Baltimore, Maryland, 1978.

MAUDEL, M.R. et al., Development and prediction of post-psychotic depression in neuroleptic-treated schizophrenics, *Arch. Gen Psychiatry, 39*, 197–203, 1982.

MAY, P.R.A. and GOLDBERG, S.C., Prediction of schizophrenic patients' response to pharmacotherapy in Lipton, M.A., DiMascio, A., and Killam, K.F. (eds.), *Psychopharmacology: A Generation of Progress*, Raven Press, New York, 1978, pp. 1139–1153.

MCGLASHAN, T.H. and CARPENTER, W.T., JR., Does attitude toward psychosis relate to outcome? *Am. J. Psychiatry, 138*:6, 797–801, 1981.

OSTOW, M., *The Psychodynamic Approach to Drug Therapy*, Psychoanalytic Research and Development Fund, New York, 1979.

Sarwer-Foner, G.L., *The Dynamics of Psychiatric Drug Therapy*, Charles C Thomas, Springfield, Illinois, 1960.

Schooler, N.R., Antipsychotic drugs and psychological treatment in schizophrenia in Lipton, M.A., DiMascio, A., and Killam, K.F. (eds.), *Psychopharmacology: A Generation of Progress*, Raven Press, New York, 1978, pp. 115–1168.

Searles, H.F., *Collected Papers on Schizophrenia and Related Subjects*, International Universities Press, New York, 1965.

Strauss, J.S. et al. (eds.), *The Psychotherapy of Schizophrenia*, Plenum Medical Book Company, New York, 1980.

Strauss, J.S. and Carpenter, W.T., Jr., *Schizophrenia*, Plenum Medical Book Company, New York, 1981.

Szymanski, H.V., Simon, J.C., and Gutterman, N., Recovery from schizophrenic psychosis, *Am. J. Psychiatry, 140*:3, 335–338, 1983.

Tamminga, C.A. and Carpenter, W.T., Jr., The DSM III diagnosis of schizophrenic-like illness and the clinical pharmacology of psychosis, *J. of Nervous and Mental Disease, 170*:12, 744–751, 1982.

Van Putten, T., Why do schizophrenic patients refuse to take their drugs? *Arch. Gen. Psychiatry, 31*, 67–72, 1974.

Van Putten, T. and May, P.R.A., Subjective response as a predictor of outcome in pharmacotherapy: the consumer has a point., *Arch. Gen. Psychiatry, 35*, 477–480, 1978.

Van Putten, T. and May, P.R.A., "Akinetic depression" in schizophrenia, *Arch. Gen. Psychiatry, 35*, 1101–1107, 1978.

Index

Acetazolamide, interaction with lithium, 35

Acutely psychotic patients, treatment of: *see* Hospitalization; Outpatient treatment of acute psychosis

Addiction, fear of, 116

Agreement, short-term treatment, 19–21

Akathisia, 37, 66

Akinesia, 66, 70

Aliphatic agents, 33

Amiloride, interaction with lithium, 35

Aminophylline, interaction with lithium, 35

Amphetamines, interaction with neuroleptics, 34

Anticholinergics, interaction with neuroleptics, 34

Antidepressants, 69
discontinuing, 145

Antidiabetic drugs, interaction with neuroleptics, 34

Antiparkinson medication, 30, 31, 36, 66, 159

Antipsychotic medication: *see* Medication

Anxiety, of therapist, 21–22

Apathy, postpsychotic: *see* Convalescence

Artane, 66

Barbiturates, interaction with neuroleptics, 34

Benztropine, 66

Bethanidine, interaction with neuroleptics, 34

Bipolar disorders
convalescence, 69
discontinuing medication, 145, 147
discussing diagnosis, 54
insight, 104, 106–107
out patient treatment, 18
prodromal symptoms, 156–159

185

Boundaries to therapeutic alliance, 55–56
Butyrophenones, 33

Caseload, 168, 169
Causes of disorder, patient's conception of, 92
Chlorpromazine, 33
Clonidine, interaction with neuroleptics, 34
Cogentin, 66
College students, problems in treatment of, 76–77
Compliance problems: see Resistance
Concentration difficulty, as promodromal symptom, 150
Concern, appropriate expression of by therapist, 19
Confidentiality, 21, 23
Consultants: see Moral objections to medication
Convalescence, 63–179
  common difficulties in distinguishing symptoms during, 70–71
  early reactions to psychotic episode, 69–70
  end of, 141–179
  initial attitudes toward outpatient treatment, 72–75
  learning from relapse, 159–160
  length of, 63, 141
  medication during: see Medication
  non-MD therapists and: see Divided treatment
  patients' questions about, 142–143
  patients' reactions to end of, 141–42
  postpsychotic apathy and depression and, 68–69, 80

psychotherapy in: see Psychotherapy
residual symptoms and, 64–65
structuring the environment during, 75–79
tardive dyskinesia, 67–68
termination of treatment and, 177–179
therapist's vacation plans and, 176–177
transition from hospital to outpatient treatment, 71–72
treatment during, 79–82
vulnerability to relapse and: see Vulnerability to relapse
Countertransference fantasies, medication as focus for, 121–122
Covert meanings of medication, 112–113, 122–125
Crisis intervention, 18, 22–23
Cyclic antidepressants, interaction with neuroleptics, 34

Debrisoquine, interaction with neuroleptics, 34
Decamethonium, interaction with lithium, 35
Deception, 21, 51
Demoralization, 69–70, 80
Denial
  assessment of vulnerability and, 89–91
  dealing with, 57–61
  early manifestations of, 4–8, 24–26
Dependence, fear of, 116
Depression
  postpsychotic, 68–69
  as prodromal symptom, 150
Diagnosis, 53–55, 131
Disagreements, between therapist and patient, dealing

with, 56–61
Distractibility, 19
Divided treatment, 127–139
  prodromal symptoms and, 172
  informal arrangements, 128–130
  structuring of, 131–136
  supervision of primary clinician in, 135–136
  transference and, 136–139
Drug interactions
  with lithium, 35
  with neuroleptics, 33
Dystonia, 30, 31, 66, 70

Educational process, 23–28
Emotional constriction, 70
Emotional stresses, of therapist, 167–169
Employers, intervention with, 23, 78
Epinephrine, interaction with neuroleptics, 34
Errors, therapist's acknowledgment of, 57
Exploratory treatment, 22, 164–176
  beginning, 164–167
  emotional stresses for the therapist and, 167–169
  prodromal symptoms and, 151–155
  psychotic experience and, 175–176
  tension between medication and, 169–174

Family
  attitude toward outpatient treatment, 74–75
  confidentiality and, 21
  denial and resistance by, 4–8, 110–120
  educational process and, 23–26
  hospitalization decision and, 10–11
  involvement of, 20
  monitoring of, 21
  outpatient treatment decision and, 9–10
  short-term treatment plan and, 20, 21
Family treatment, 80, 81
Fluphenazine, 33
Furosemide, interaction with lithium, 55

Guanethidine, interaction with neuroleptics, 34
Guarded patients, 19

Haldol, 33
Haloperidol, 33
  interaction with lithium, 35
High school students, convalescent environment for, 75–76
Hospital emergency room clinicians, referral by, 6
Hospitalization, 1–2, 8–14
  discussing, 10–11
  managing transition to hospital, 11–14
  vs. outpatient treatment, 8–10
  refusal of medication and, 40
  transition to outpatient treatment and, 71–72
Hypomania, as prodromal symptom, 149, 156–158; *see also* Bipolar disorders
Hypnotics, interaction with neuroleptics, 34

Ibuprofen, interaction with lithium, 35
Indomethacin, interaction with lithium, 35

Informed consent, 3, 27, 68
Initial visit, preparation for, 3–5
Insight
   dimensions of, 89–94
   fragility of, 157
   patterns of, 94–107
Insulin
   interaction with lithium, 35
   interaction with neuroleptics, 34
Intellectual functioning, 64–65, 75
Iproniazid, interaction with neuroleptics, 34

Jargon, 22, 24, 53–54

Language, 24, 26–27, 53–54
L-dopa, interaction with neuroleptics, 34
Lithium
   drug interactions with, 35
   side effects of, 67

Manic patients: *see* Bipolar disorders
Medical model, 109–112
Medication
   anticipatory, 170–174
   choosing, 31–35
   clinically significant drug interactions with lithium, 35
   clinically significant drug interactions with neuroleptics, 34
   commonly prescribed neuroleptics, 33
   consent to use of, 18
   cost of, 32
   covert meanings of, 112–113, 122–125
   definition of role of, after convalescence, 143
   discontinuing, 144–147

   in divided treatment, 128–136
   dosage, 31–32, 117, 145–147
   dystonic reactions and, 30, 31
   early subjective reactions to, 32, 34, 36–39
   educational process and, 27–28
   as embodiment of psychotic illness, 116–118
   explaining purpose of, 26–28
   fear of addiction to, 116
   as focus for transference and countertransference fantasies, 120–122
   informed consent and, 27, 68
   intermittent, 37, 147–148
   moral objections to, 113–116
   negative subjective reactions to, 36–38
   patients' attitudes toward, 25, 28–30, 32, 34, 36–39, 70, 109–112
   patients' conceptions of nature and efficacy of, 92–93
   patients' self-management of, 160–161
   positive subjective reactions to, 34, 36
   refusal of, 39–43
   resistance to, 24–26, 28–31, 110–120
   risks, timing of discussion of, 27
   side effects of, 29, 65–67, 70–71, 80–81
   tardive dyskinesia and, 67–68, 161–163
   tension between exploratory treatment and, 169–174
   traditional medical model and, 109–112
Mellaril, 33
Methyldopa, interaction with lithium, 35

Misinformation, fears resulting from, 112
Moral objections to medication, 113–116
   need for second opinion, 115–116

Naproxen, interaction with lithium, 35
Narcotics, interaction with neuroleptics, 34
Navane, 33
Negative transference, medication as focus for, 120–121
Neuroleptic agents; *see also* Medication
   choosing, 31–34
   clinically significant drug interactions with, 34
   commonly prescribed, 33
   discontinuing, 145
Non-MD therapist–psychiatrist relationship: *see* Divided treatment
Nurse-clinician–psychiatrist relationship: *see* Divided treatment

Outpatient treatment of acute psychosis, 1–61
   approaching the patient, 18–19
   as crisis intervention, 18, 22–23
   educational process in, 23–28
   vs. hospitalization, 8–10
   indications for, 17, 18
   informed consent and, 27
   initial visit, preparation for, 3–5
   medication in: *see* Medication
   non-MD therapists and: *see* Divided treatment
   practical advice on short-term management of patient's affairs, 23

short-term treatment agreement and, 19–21
sources of referral and, 5–6
tasks in, 17–18
termination, 177–179
therapeutic alliance and: *see* Therapeutic alliance
therapist's anxiety and, 21–22
therapist's vacations and, 176

Pancuronium, interaction with lithium, 35
Patient-therapist relationship: *see* Therapeutic alliance
Perphenazine, 33
Phenylbutazone, interaction with lithium, 35
Physical restraint, 13
Piperazine, 33
Piperidine, 33
Piroxicam, interaction with lithium, 35
Preoccupation, as prodromal symptom, 150
Privacy of clinician, 50–52, 56
Prodromal symptoms of psychosis, 148–161
   exploration of, 151–155
   identification of, 148–151
   vs. resistance symptoms, 170–173
   timing of, 158–159
Prolixin, 33
Psychotherapy
   after convalescence, 163–164
   during convalescence, 80–82
   definition of role of, after convalescence, 143–144
   in divided treatment, 129–139
   exploratory: *see* Exploratory treatment
   moral objections to, 114
   resistance to medication and,

118–119
  termination of, 177–179
Psychiatrist–non-MD therapist
  relationship: *see* Divided
  treatment
Psychotic episodes
  early reactions to, 69–70
  prodromal symptoms and: *see*
    Prodromal symptoms of psy-
    chosis
Psychotic symptoms
  capacity to acknowledge and
    describe, 90–91
  denial of, 4–8
  exploratory treatment and,
    170–171
  hospitalization vs. outpatient
    treatment and, 8–9
  residual, 64–65
  resistance, 170–173
  target, 26–27

Referral, sources of, 5–6
Relapse
  learning from, 159–160
  vulnerability to: *see* Vulnerabil-
    ity to relapse
Reserpine, interaction with
  neuroleptics, 34
Residual symptoms, 64–65
Resistance
  early manifestations of, 4–8,
    24–26
  to hospitalization, 12
  to medication, 24–26, 28–31,
    110–120
  therapeutic alliance and, 48,
    59–61
Resistance symptoms, 170–173

Safety of patient, 13–14, 17, 20
Scheduling patients, 168
Schizophrenia, 54

School, return to, 75–77
School authorities, intervention
  with, 23, 75–76
Sedation, 65
Self-assessment of vulnerability,
  84, 86–89
Short-term treatment agreement,
  19–21
Sleep disturbance, as prodromal
  symptom, 149, 152
Social withdrawal, as prodromal
  symptom, 149–150
Social worker–psychiatrist relationship: *see* Divided treatment
Sodium bicarbonate, interaction
  with lithium, 35
Sodium chloride, interaction
  with lithium, 35
Spectinomycin, interraction with
  lithium, 35
Spironolactone, interaction with
  lithium, 35
Stalemate as global resistance,
  118–120
Stelazine, 33
Stresses, for therapist, 167–169
  access to colleagues for discus-
    sion, 169
  balanced case load, 168–169
  countertransference, 168
  scheduling difficult patients,
    168
  supervision by senior clinician,
    169
Succinylcholine, interaction with
  lithium, 35
Sulindac, interaction with lithium, 35
Supervision of therapist, by senior clinician
  in divided treatment, 135–136
  to ease stress, 169

Suspiciousness, as prodromal symptom, 149–150

Tardive dyskinesia, 67–68, 161–163
Target symptoms, of psychosis, 26–27
Termination, 177–179
Tetracycline, interaction with lithium, 35
Theophylline, interaction with lithium, 35
Therapeutic alliance, 45–61
  acute crisis and, 22
  building, 45–49
  confidentiality and, 3
  curiosity about therapist and, 50–52
  dealing with major disagreements, 56–61
  establishing a therapeutic atmosphere, 49–51
  hospitalization decision and, 9, 12–13
  informed consent and, 3
  limits and boundaries to, 55–56
  talking with patients, 51–55
Thiazide diuretics, interaction with lithium, 35
Thioridazine, 33, 67
Thiothixene, 33
Thioxanthene, 33

Transference
  divided, 136–139
  medication as focus for, 120–122
Transport to hospital, 11–12
Triamterene, interaction with lithium, 35
Trifluoperazine, 33
Trihexyphenidyl, 66
Trilafon, 33
Trust, 129

Urea, interaction with lithium, 35

Vacations, therapist's, 176–177
Vulnerability to relapse, 26, 83–107
  biologic, 84–85
    case examples, 95–96, 99, 101
  control of, 147–159
  dimensions of insight, 89–94
  patterns of insight, 94–107
  psychologic, 85–86
    case examples, 95, 99, 101, 103
  self-assessment of, 84, 86–89

Work, return to, 78–79

Zomepirac, interaction with lithium, 35